First published by Kesho Publishers Ltd., 1986
London, England.

ISBN 0-908305-01-X

A version of this book was published in Germany: Ruth Weiss,
Die Frauen von Zimbabwe, München: Weismann Verlag-Frauenbuchverlag, 1983.

Printed by Aldgate Press, 84B Whitechapel High St, London E1

The Women of Zimbabwe

Ruth Weiss

Kesho Publications

For the unsung African woman

CONTENTS

About the Author

Ruth Weiss has written extensively on the economic problems and history of the underdeveloped nations, particularly those in Africa. As a child, she fled with her parents from the Germany of the 1930s to South Africa, where she lived for 30 years. She then worked in Zimbabwe during the period of UDI, running the Salisbury Bureau of the *Financial Mail*, but was deported after two years by the Rhodesian régime. She joined the staff of the *Guardian* in London, and then returned to Africa as business editor of the *Times of Zambia* and the Zambian correspondent for the *Financial Times*. Since then, she has chiefly worked as a freelance writer and broadcaster, but returned to Zimbabwe in 1982 to spend two years training young journalists. Her publications include: *Strategic Highways of Africa* (Julian Friedmann, 1977); *South Africa* (Swedish Institute of International Affairs, 1977); contributions to *Rhodesiens Zukunft heisst Zimbabwe* (Verlag Otto Lembeck, 1977) and to Suedliches Africa *(ed. P. Ripken, Wagenbach, 1978); Ein Lied Ohne Musik*, a political autobiography (Laetare, 1981); *Afrika den Europaern*, written with Hans Mayer (Peter Hammer Verlag, 1984); and the script for the film *South Africa Belongs to Us*, a portrait of five South African women, which was released in 1980. She has also written *An Introduction to Economic Reporting in Africa*, which will be published by the African Council of Communication Education (Nairobi) in 1986.

Introduction

It is hardly surprising that women have played a role — in some cases are still playing a role — in the liberation wars of Africa. Women, after all, had a very specific and a very special role in traditional society and it was this society that was raped, if not destroyed, by colonialism. The woman suffered badly, often becoming a worse victim than the man. The Black woman of South Africa is, sadly, an excellent example — for she is at the very bottom of the apartheid ladder. She is oppressed, because all Blacks are oppressed; she is exploited, because all Blacks are exploited. But she is also exploited because she is a woman: first, by the Whites, who force her to accept the humblest jobs by allowing her even less education than that offered to men; and second, by her man, because his superior position as a male is about all that is left of the traditional structure of society.

Women in Southern Africa often say, 'we know our men treat us badly, we know that we are minors all our lives, and we know that we must change all this. But for the moment we are together in the struggle. We cannot fight a divided struggle, the way European women want us to, fighting for sexual equality. This means nothing to us when we are all exploited, simply because of our colour.' Black women took up arms with their men in many countries: a long time ago in Algeria and, until recently, in Angola, Guinea Bissau, Mozambique and Zimbabwe. Today, they are still struggling to throw off the yoke of oppression in Namibia and South Africa.

This book is about the Women of Zimbabwe, whose struggle for freedom ended so very recently, in 1979/80. Their active and often dangerous support for ZANLA (the Zimbabwean African National Liberation Army, the military wing of ZANU, the party led by Robert Mugabe) and ZIPRA (the Zimbabwe People's Liberation Army, the armed wing of ZAPU, led by Joshua Nkomo) was a major contribution to the victory of the nation's Black majority. But what, I wondered, had happened after the war? What had given these women, the young and the old, the educated and the illiterate, the strength to fight the White man and his rule? What, I wondered, would be the role of women in the new Zimbabwe — and what had been their role under British colonialism and the illegal Smith régime?

As a journalist, I travelled through the country and asked these questions. In these pages, I have tried to tell the story of the Women in Zimbabwe who, to use their own words, have carried a heavy load. If I have erred, the fault is mine entirely. I believe that many women still carry a heavy load; but I believe, too, that the load is being lightened, thanks to the social change that was set in motion by the armed revolution in which women themselves played such a dynamic role.

Nehanda

Where would we be,
People of Zimbabwe,
without you?

Leader, Spirit, Mother!
Mbuya, we are yours.

Mbuya Nehanda, she is the one,
She leads us, she
It is Who gives us
Strength.

My pride is your pride,
My power is your power.
Mbuya Nehanda.

You who suffered
You who fought
You who died —

You are our spirit
Our guide
Our unity

Like you, I know
We will triumph
and —
Like you
We will never surrender.

Elizabeth

A meeting of the Ruzane Literary Group in 1983. In order to finance their project, the group grows and sells vegetables — here they are standing next to a crop of onions they have grown together.

1

AGENTS OF POLITICAL CHANGE

Jane Ngwenya

Jane Ngwenya was born on the 15 June, 1935, in the Buhera district. Since her mother was a Shona from the Chiwata area, her grandfather belonged to the Makorekore, and her father came from Basutoland, she was able to speak the languages of both Mashonaland and Matabeleland fluently from childhood — which was a great advantage. Mrs Ngwenya's mother was unusual for one of her generation, in that she could read and write, and she was determined that Jane and her other daughter should be well educated. Fortunately, although her first husband died when Jane was young, her second husband supported her in this endeavour. Jane first went to a local school and then, helped by her grandmother, who paid for her uniform and school fees, was sent to a boarding school. She left school in 1952 and immediately started teaching.

Jane married young; this she says, is where her problems began.

Unfortunately, my husband couldn't stand my political attitude. He wanted a traditional woman, a woman who would not do anything that her husband doesn't want. A woman who would only take orders from her husband. I'm afraid I became an odd woman.

I was an ordinary primary school teacher. I earned very little money, £3 17s 6d. It was then increased to £5 and teachers were among the highest paid people. But I am an argumentative person. I wanted to know why we were paid so little when White teachers with the same qualifications, or even lower qualifications than ourselves, were being paid so much more.

I was one of the teachers who were elected as a delegate to an African Teachers' Association Conference. At the conference I was not submissive at all. I spoke about our grievances. I also objected to the attitude of the President of our Teachers' Association. I realised that he was one of the most brainwashed people. He always spoke well of the government. He never complained about the differential in salary between Black and White teachers.

In those days, people were frightened if you spoke out. They thought you had lost your prestige. You were only popular if you were submissive. But although I was born into the Church and went to church regularly, I felt that we were being brainwashed. I had a few good White friends to whom I talked and they understood what I was saying. They realised the injustice of it all. The more I spoke out, the less popular I became, and I knew that there was no solution, that I had to resign from teaching before I became 'black'-listed because of being so outspoken.

So I gave up teaching and went to South Africa to learn dressmaking. After that I became self-employed. I was happily married but then I began to attend political meetings seriously. My husband became jealous, I think. Not simply because I was more active than he was, but also because there were only men, or mostly men, at these meetings. Very often, I was the only woman. I could name a few other women of my time, Mrs Mushandi, Mrs Mushonga, Mrs Murape, Mrs Makwavarara and others. We were a handful of women.

The more active I became in politics, the more difficulties I had in my marriage. My husband hated me going to meetings. He used to beat me up. And unfortunately, he had the support of my relatives. They used to say, 'You cannot have a man being dictated to by a woman. A woman must stay at home.' So when he was cruel to me, and beat me, no one helped me. One day, he beat me unconscious and I landed up in hospital. In the end, I realised that divorce was the only answer. My two children were very small at the time and my husband insisted that he should keep them. Fortunately, he allowed me to see them regularly and he brought them to see me.

In 1960, I became really active, politically speaking. That was the year that the NDP Congress was held and, to my surprise, I was elected to the leadership. This was the beginning of the continued series of arrests and detentions. From that time on, I was in and out of prison five times before I was detained permanently. After that, I stayed in prison for over nine years. I used to send money to my mother for my children and in 1964, Christian Care began to give help to all the detainees. As well, Amnesty International and other groups adopted us.

I think I became politicised when I was very small. It is difficult to say, but you always knew that you were worse off than the White children. I always wanted to feel free and independent. I'm not friendly with everyone who happens to be Black. I choose my friends, whatever their colour. Well, when I was small, I wanted to play with other children. I wanted to play the sort of games that

Whites played. But there was always the colour bar. White children wouldn't be allowed to play with me. At school, I felt bad when we were told, 'Mrs So-and-So is coming. You must dress very smartly.' I used to feel, 'Why should I dress more smartly just because a White woman is coming to see us?' I felt the same when a White minister of religion came to preach in our church and everything had to be made very special. I asked myself, 'Don't we pray to the same God?'

I feel the same way about men. I mean, there is nothing wrong with being gentle with a man, but I think that there are some aspects of our tradition which should be changed. A woman should not be repressed simply because she is a woman, just as a Black person should not be oppressed simply because he or she is Black.

It was the rural woman, the ordinary uneducated woman, who took a lead in the sixties. The women's demonstrations started after our leaders were arrested. When Michael Mawema and the Takawiras were arrested, it was the women who demonstrated. I think women felt not only more oppressed, but also very much more aware of the situation than many men. We came out and demonstrated. We were bitten by dogs. We were beaten up by the police with batons. We suffered all sorts of things. This happened not only in Salisbury [now Harare] and in Bulawayo, but all over the country, from Umtali [Mutari] to Plumtree. All the demonstrations were spontaneous.

Our leaders here were arrested and later, leaders were also arrested in Nyasaland [now Malawi] and Northern Rhodesia [Zambia]. They were brought to prison here in Southern Rhodesia, in Salisbury and Gwelo [now Gweru]. The women were talking about the culling of the cattle, about the land, about the fact that the children had no schools to go to, about the taxes and so many other things. You have no idea how tremendous the response was when the NDP was formed. I was a founder member of the nationalist movement, as you know, and at first we were so pleased when we had 25 to 30 people. But once the NDP was formed, then you could say that 1,000 was a small gathering. We used to have something like 60,000 to 90,000 people coming to a meeting. That was what the spirit was like in those days. What I feel deserves to be mentioned, is that most of the women who came to our meetings and our demonstrations were uneducated, rural women. They were very strong. It was not difficult to encourage them to fight for their rights. The educated women felt threatened. They had been brainwashed. They had something to lose if they were politically active. It was only in the sixties, really, that the educated women started to be as active as the uneducated. In the early days, they used to look down on us, they used to laugh because we were dancing and ululating. After all, they were trying to get away from this kind of thing, the traditional way of doing things. They wanted to become like the White madam.

But you know, eventually everybody realised that the White madams didn't care how any Black behaved. They still remained 'Kaffirs'.

Mrs Ngwenya was first elected to an executive post in 1959. Because she had a small baby at the time, she says, she escaped the brutality of the police. But she was frequently beaten later on. In 1964, when she was serving her prison sentence in Gwcru, the savage treatment of the police caused permanent damage to one of her kidneys, to the point where it no longer functions. In 1971, she was released and went into exile. She lived for some time in Zambia, where she was responsible for the women in the refugee and guerrilla camps run by ZAPU. In 1979, she returned home, where she continued her political work for ZAPU. She stood for election in 1980 and became a Member of Parliament. In 1982, she was appointed to the position of Deputy Minister of Manpower Planning, which she held until June 1985.

Julia Zvobgo

Another woman who was active in the early days of the struggle is Mrs Julia Zvobgo. She was born in Shurugwi (also the home of Ian Smith) into a polygamous family. Luckily for her, her father believed that girls were as likely as boys to benefit from an education. Having moved away from Shurugwi to start a small business near Beit Bridge in the south of the country, he sent Julia to boarding school. At the time, she was planning to attend a teacher's training college and become a teacher. But in 1961, she married Eddison Zvobgo (who is today the Minister of Justice, Parliamentary and Legal Affairs) and so remained at home. Shortly afterwards, he left to study in the United States.

Like her husband, Julia was active in politics as a member of the NDP.

In the early sixties, there were demonstrations, women's demonstrations all over the country. Many of the women suffered dog bites. We had thought that although men had been set on by dogs and beaten by the police, or sent to prison, they would not punish women in the same way. There was another point. We knew that men who were politically active and demonstrated could lose their jobs, but few of us women had jobs. I was pregnant at the time and when they set the dogs on us, they left me alone. They did not even arrest me although they were arresting and hitting people all around me; it was funny, leaving me standing there. If you look at the photographs of that time, you can see them hitting people all around me. I think the work that women did during this time was really powerful, because it was through this sort of demonstration that our women realised that they were not useless, that it was possible for them to do something. Many of these women could not even understand English, and they couldn't read or write. Before the demonstrations, they would say, 'Oh, we can't do this.' But afterwards, there was a tremendous strength and spirit among all the women.

I myself had my baby and subsequently went to Fort Victoria [Masvingo] to try and get a job as a teacher. This was in 1964. Eddison was already back and I knew that he would be arrested, so I thought the best thing would be to leave Salisbury. So I went to Fort Victoria. And, of course, I was right. Eddison was arrested. As a result I couldn't get a job. The authorities argued that I was politically involved and therefore should not have a Civil Servant's job.

My father-in-law had a school that he had started himself and he wanted me to work for him, but he realised there would be problems. So in the end, I decided to go to my parents and help my father in his shop. Nearby there was a Catholic school and they wanted me to come and teach, but I told the priest that I would not be allowed to come. He told me to fill in the forms and see what happened. Well, naturally, I was turned down, but the priest went as far as the court, arguing that I myself had never been arrested. In the end, he got his way and I was allowed to work there. It was a difficult time for us — Eddison had been detained and people were being sent to prison at Gonakudzingwa.

At this time, I began to study for my secondary school teacher's certificate. I always studied at night. Then, in 1968, I left the country; I stayed out until after the Lancaster House negotiations in 1979. I went to London first. Eddison left after the Pearce Commission in 1971 and we then went to the United States together, where he studied.

At first, I did nothing. I wanted to be a mother and a wife. Don't forget, the children's father had been in detention for a very long time, almost 10 years, and they hardly knew him. I had a difficult job trying to make them understand each other. The children didn't know what a father was and didn't know how to behave towards him. And the father didn't know how to behave towards his children. So I thought I should try and stay at home. But I soon became bored and started studying political science. I got my Master's degree and then studied business administration.

In 1977, Mrs Zvobgo went to Mozambique, where she worked mainly with women. After her return to Zimbabwe in 1979, she stood for Parliament and was elected. She became the treasurer of a new organisation, the Zimbabwe National Women's Organisation, which was an attempt to forge an umbrella body for all women's organisations. Today, she is an office bearer in the executive of the Women's League of ZANU, holding the publicity portfolio.

The efforts of women like Mrs Zvobgo and Mrs Ngwenya in the sixties were only the beginning of a long struggle. In 1964, the Rhodesian Front, which opposed all change and all concessions to Blacks, displaced its first leader in favour of Ian Smith. He began a drawn-out game of cat and mouse with the British Government. The latter, both in theory and in terms of the constitution, was still responsible for the welfare of the Black Southern Rhodesians — in much the same way that it is presently responsible for the welfare of the Falkland Islanders. Smith and his followers, reluctant to grant real political rights to Blacks and denying them any genuine economic advancement, warned Whitehall that they would take matters into their own hands, 'to preserve civilised standards'. In 1964, both African parties were banned. Leaders such as Nkomo, Sithole, Mugabe and Tekere, were detained.

Then, on 11 November, 1965, despite a visit to Southern Rhodesia by the British Prime Minister, Ian Smith illegally and unilaterally declared his country's independence. The Unilateral Declaration of Independence (UDI) that was signed by the Smith Cabinet reads like a copy of the Declaration of Independence made by the United States in 1776. There, however, the similarity ends. The Americans were fighting British colonialism; but Smith and the Rhodesian Front were fighting to preserve all White privileges for a mere quarter of a million Whites — at the expense of almost seven million Blacks.

It was not long before open conflict erupted between the Black majority and the White minority, as Blacks sought to gain what was rightfully theirs: full participation in the political affairs of their own country. But because of Smith's intransigence and the Whites'

Comrade Jane Ngwenya.

Comrade Sally Mugabe.

Comrade Julia Zvobgo.

self-seeking belief in his leadership and in the rightness of their cause, it took some 15 years and thousands of lives to reach this goal.

Sally Mugabe

"It's very exciting...I just can't express it...20 years of struggle!" That was Mrs Sally Mugabe's reaction when I asked her to comment on the results of the elections in March 1980, which brought Independence to Zimbabwe and made her husband, Robert Mugabe, the Prime Minister of his country — after 20 years of struggle. Women like Mrs Mugabe had fought not only against the unfair domination of the Black majority, but also for the equality of women with men. The issue of women's rights, she believes, is still a very important issue.

Her office is not in a plush, high-rise office block in the centre of Harare, but at 88 Manica Road, on the edge of the Black commercial area. This building, the headquarters of ZANU (PF), witnesses the constant stream of Black workers entering and leaving the city every day. It was besieged by African supporters during the run-up to the election period and immediately after Independence, and is still a hub of activity. To get to Mrs Mugabe's office, one has to pass not only the people crowding round the entrance, but also tight security. Such security is necessary. In 1981, a bomb destroyed part of the building — another of South Africa's efforts to destabilise its neighbours. Some people were killed, many were injured. The top of the building was blown off, but Mrs Mugabe and the other staff are still working there.

Upstairs in the tiny cubicle which serves as her office, she is interviewing a group of women who have just returned to Zimbabwe after 18 months in Cuba. These are rural women, who have never before had the benefit of education or travel. Their horizon has been widened and Sally Mugabe listens quietly as they talk of their experiences. She is very content with her job. For it affords her the greatest possible satisfaction: she could have been in Parliament, but gave up her seat so that a rural woman could be elected in her stead.

In 1977, she was appointed to the second position within the Women's Department of the Party. The first position was taken by Mrs Teurai Ropa Nhongo, the Minister for women's affairs. In 1984, Mrs Mugabe was confirmed as the woman responsible for the Women's Department of the Party, which she organises with great efficiency and dedication; at the same time, she was elected as a member of the ZANU (PF) Central Committee.

Mrs Mugabe was born in Ghana, where she met Robert Mugabe when he was working there as a teacher. She, too, is a teacher. In 1980, she came to Southern Rhodesia, where they married. She immediately became involved in politics and rose to leadership in her own right. She was active in the women's demonstrations of the 1960s and was one of the founding members of ZANU. She is a woman who has known great sorrow. She was separated from her husband for a long time while he was in prison — he was not released until 1974. She, too, was imprisoned. As well, she suffered the tragic loss of her young son, and another child died in childbirth. Yet she is not bitter. She is a woman who feels that it is her duty to lead and to set an example through work. She dislikes being interviewed now. She feels that she has said all there is to say. What counts now, she says, are her actions: the work she does for and with women, in an effort to improve their standard of living and to teach them the skills that will make them more economically independent.

Her West African background, she says, has been a help to her. In 1979, she told me:

> African women had a very strong position. They were the mothers, the bread-winners, the organisers, the wives of the husbands, all at the same time. The family depended on the women for food, money, comfort, many things. It gave them a powerful position in the family, in the tribe and in the village. But they were, of course, handicapped. They couldn't take decisions — they couldn't decide about marriage or funeral arrangements, or even about festivals. There was little justice in that. Women tried to speak out at village meetings against some of these things, but with little success. The men feel that they are in a superior position, so the women have to fight for their rights on a collective basis...they cannot do it on their own. Women talk about these things amongst themselves when they are washing at the riverside, shopping at the market, or cooking at home.

> In West Africa, the women moved from this very traditional state to a higher level. I think that this was because our colonialism was not the same as in Southern Africa. We didn't have the settlers. We had Europeans who came to work in Africa, but they never actually settled. In Southern Africa, they found that the weather was good and that there were large areas which they could occupy. Then they decided to settle, forcing the people into subservience and manipulating them. These things worked against the women, the Black women of Southern Africa. We in West Africa — it was easier for us to do things for ourselves.

> In Ghana, we knew that we were oppressed by the colonialists who had come into our country. It was not the sort of oppression that

made us hate the White man. Luckily, we had the American, George Padmore. He talked to us about this oppression and made things very clear to us. He educated us. We, the women of Ghana, knew that women should be free, and attended rallies and seminars regularly so as to learn about the message which Padmore had brought to us.

As time went on, things changed. We realised that we had to be a new people. We had to have an African personality. We would be Ghanaians, we would be masters in our own home. And, of course, we were very proud that we women played a great part in bringing Nkrumah, the man who brought real freedom to Ghana, to power.

After independence in Ghana, women formed organisations and continued to teach the people about politics, economics, about their own social situation. Really, this was a great help to women. Even uneducated women took it upon themselves to attend meetings. It was such a big thing. Everyone wanted to be seen to be in politics. It went on for a very long time.

As soon as I arrived in Southern Africa, I was shocked at the condition of the women. I immediately became involved and I am very pleased that women have come as far as they have. Women carrying the gun in the war — this was very important. Women will help Zimbabwe to develop into a prosperous country where people have educated and disciplined minds: this will help in the development of the country. Women must be involved in the general process of development. They must not lag behind. They have learned a lot in the struggle through the war.

Mrs Mugabe is helping them to learn what they can. She works tirelessly, despite the illness which struck her down and forced her to undergo treatment overseas during 1983. There is no corner of the country that is not of interest to her, no area where she has not been to rallies, where she has not spoken to women. She also works hard to help her husband, and is one of his valued advisors. Whether one talks to her in her little office in Manica Road, follows her to one of her many meetings, or sees her walking in the grounds of the Prime Ministerial residence, one knows that this is a woman who was not only born, but is prepared, to lead, despite the tremendous strain that this means for her.
In 1979, she spoke of the change that had come about in the status of women as a result of the war:

Women are really appreciative of the changes that have come and they want these changes to continue. And the men, too, are always asking to meet with the women to discuss problems. The thing is, that not only are women ignorant about men — men are also ignorant about women. We must educate them. The men must learn to understand our physique. Obviously, there are certain handicaps. We have different biological make-ups. We must explain this to the men. At the same time, we must learn about them. This exchange of ideas has already yielded good results. One saw it in the camps. It was interesting to see both men and women sitting down to discuss problems. They discussed, for example, what should happen when a woman became pregnant: what should happen to her, and what should happen to the child. If you see comrades discussing this sort of thing, then you know that things have changed. It could never have happened if it hadn't been for the war. It is a whole transformation, both for men and for women. Things have changed because of the struggle and they must continue to change.

Teurai Ropa Nhongo

The young Teurai Ropa Nhongo fought alongside men in the struggle for liberation. Her 'Chimurenga'[1] name, in fact, means 'spill blood'. Today she is married, busy raising a family and holding down a job, like many other women in Zimbabwe. But this 31 year old has a very special job: she is the Minister in the Cabinet who is responsible for women's affairs. As Zimbabwe's youngest Minister, Mrs Nhongo is as committed to her present work as she was to the struggle.

She was born in 1955 as Joyce Mugari, at Chawanda village, Mount Darwin, and went to school at the Howard Institute in the Mazoe area. Then, after passing her Form 2 in 1973, she joined the liberation struggle. She received basic training before being assigned to field operations, and arrived in Zambia in 1974. In the same year, she became a member of the General Staff of ZANLA and Commander of ZANLA's Women's Detachment when it was formed. A year later, she was moved from Zambia to Mozambique as a political instructor. In 1976, she was made Commander of Mozambique's Chimoio camp, the largest refugee camp in the country. She also met and married the camp's military commander, Rex Nhongo, who is today the head of Zimbabwe's national army. In 1977, Mrs Nhongo became a member of the Central Committee and was appointed Secretary of Women's Affairs; she was the first woman ever to be appointed to ZANU's National Executive of the Central Committee. She held this position until 1980, when she was elected to represent the Mashonaland Central Constituency.

Kate Truscott

This woman, a member of the Ruzane Literary group in Wedza, has learnt to read, write and do basic arithmetic in the years since Independence.

The Minister not only talks of women's rights and the need for improvement — she leads the way. Since she left school after Form 2, she felt the need for further education and, despite her overwhelming workload and her family duties, began to study for O' levels (which she has now passed). It is understandable, therefore, that she welcomed the decision to move Adult Literacy from the Ministry of Education to her own. She believed that this fitted in with some of the programmes already initiated. Women, after all, are the largest group of illiterates in the country: at least 60% of rural women cannot read or write. 'This is their biggest problem,' said Minister Nhongo. 'To be a success, we need literate women, who should be able to read and write so that they can plan. Everything starts by being able to do things for oneself.' Literacy, she added, will also decrease the dependency of women on their men. For once a woman is educated, she can make plans for herself and is enabled to see — and to seize — opportunities of gainful work in her own environment, so that she will not have to move elsewhere.

The Minister is painfully aware of women's problems. She knows that African women all over the continent suffer not only from a lack of confidence, but also from traditional handicaps: marrying young, having too many children too quickly, working too hard both in the fields and in the home, and being given few opportunities for education and employment. And in Zimbabwe, there was the added dimension of racial discrimination: the Black man became the unskilled labourer in the modern cash economic sector, caught up in the invidious system of migrant labour, which turned the woman into a grass widow for most of the year. This gave her added work and new responsibilities for the husband's family in his absence. With the young men away, the rural areas were peopled by women, children and older people, and the workload fell on the shoulders of the younger women. If women did drift to the towns in search of their men, stability, or job opportunities, they entered the labour market at the bottom of the ladder: the lowest paid and the least appreciated of the labour force, in the factories and the White households. Even in industry, which had a minimum wage, a woman worker usually received a sum slightly less than the minimum.

Zimbabwean women had a further problem: the colonial laws differentiated between a White person's marriage and that of an African. A woman married according to customary or 'Christian' rites fell under the Native Marriage Act (later amended to the African Marriage Act), and became a minor all her life, subject to the tutelage of a father, husband, or uncle. Mrs Nhongo was one of the people who lobbied for the Legal Age of Majority Act, which was passed in December 1982. Many have called this law the opening shot in the struggle for the liberation of Zimbabwe's women: the first shot, because a woman is now able to do things on her own. She can now open a bank account, enter into contracts and make her own decisions. As no changes have as yet been made to the provision of the Marriage Act and customary law, however, women revert to the status of minors after marriage — an anomaly which needs to be changed.

At the Women's Day rally in Harare on 8 March 1983, Minister Nhongo urged all women to press for their rights. She told the meeting that the goal of Zimbabwe as a developing socialist state was equality for all citizens before the law. She said, 'Women participated in the national liberation struggle for human rights, and their resources must be made full use of in a mutually complementary manner rather than in a master-servant relationship which smacks of exploitation of one group by the other'.

On the same occasion, she urged women to join trade unions. Women, she said, could do as well as men if they were only given the chance. 'But in Harare,' she added, 'out of 86 councillors, only two are women, and Bulawayo has none. In Parliament, the body that represents the whole society, there are only 12 women out of 140.' She pointed out, too, that although the government was the largest employer of labour, no woman yet sat on the Public Services Commission.[2] 'These are the areas which we need to transform,' she said.

She also spoke of the new Majority Act and asked women to 'adopt positive and progressive attitudes and to show a fighting spirit for equality, justice and human rights.' Some aspects of customary law needed change, she said, to protect women from such injustices as eviction from their homes and the loss of property after the death of their husbands. She added that while other Ministries such as Home Affairs, Justice, or Legal and Parliamentary Affairs, were responsible for the administration of various laws affecting women, there were researchers in her own Ministry who were reviewing legislation which conflicted with 'what government expects of us'. Such research, she explained, covers the marriage laws. She also commented that the question of income tax was under review; many women, she said, felt that they were unfairly treated by the present regulations.

She does not think that women are without male support. While it was true that men were in control of most institutions, she said, it was evident that they, too, accepted change. 'Because of the war experience, some men have realised that they can't do anything without the involvement of women. They saw their participation during the war and this is why we have very few problems in this Ministry.' She added that because of the war, it was easy to explain matters to people and to receive positive responses. As for the women who had been in the war, some, she said, had been unhappy after their return, but realised that in order to improve their position, they needed to further their education. Many, she said, had attended academic courses and acquired satisfactory positions. 'It is difficult to satisfy the whole country,' she added, 'but one tries.'

Asked if the changes had come too rapidly for the older people, Minister Nhongo commented that the young had to realise that their views were different and that the older people needed time to adjust. 'We have to take issues very simply, so that we do not get strong opposition from the people who should give us support.' Things should be taken in stages and the people made to understand what is required of them. She felt that the advice of experts — sociologists, for instance — would be invaluable, so that change would be introduced at the right time and with the right touch.

There is evidence that the Minister's concern for women has been translated into action. The Ministry, which services a major community development programme throughout the country, has organised hundreds of workshops on many issues affecting women and has issued a survey on the situation of women in the country. The numerous women's clubs and organisations, as well as the constant debate on women's affairs in the columns of the media, are visible signs of the Minister's dedication. She has often stated that Independence requires even greater efforts: a dictum that is well appreciated by those who see a woman in the prime of her life contributing so much to the lives of others.

Pamela

Women in the urban areas were less exposed to the war, the security forces and the fighting, than the women on the land. As a result, few women from places such as Salisbury joined the struggle. Pamela, however, did. While she was a junior nurse, she explained, a wounded soldier had been brought in, accompanied by men of the security forces. She became curious about this case, because no one was allowed to see his medical record and because the security people never left him. Her curiosity got the better of her. By volunteering to change bandages (a job which everyone hated) on the grounds that she was keen to learn more about nursing, she was able to spend some time with the prisoner. She ensured a measure of privacy by telling the security guards that they must go away while she changed the dressings.

The young man began to trust her. He told her that he had been the commander of a group which had successfully ambushed Rhodesian forces and killed many men. He himself had been wounded and taken prisoner. After a while, he began to tell her about the war and the reasons for the struggle. She became convinced that she was nursing the wrong people. It was not so easy in Salisbury to find out what was happening but once she knew, nothing could stop her. She started by bringing small gifts of oranges and other food to the wounded prisoner. Eventually her plans matured and one night, she slipped away and made her way to the rural areas, where she joined the liberation movement.

Dorothy

I was working in the fields when my brother came. He was five years old and he should have been with the other boys, looking after the cattle and my mother's goats. So I walked with Chisi, my younger sister, to the anthill where he was waiting.

'The comrades,' he said. He was so excited that he could hardly speak...his thin legs kept moving, and he waved his arms. He kept repeating, 'The comrades,' without saying anything more. Impatiently, I said, 'Show me,' but he ran so fast that I had trouble keeping up with him. It was almost time to leave the fields — the darkness was not far away. I remembered Chisi and ran back to fetch her. I put her on my back, because she was too young to run fast.

My brother skirted the path from the village and went towards a place which girls like me had never visited. Granite rocks, placed carefully by the *vadzimu* [ancestors], were sitting one on top of the other, with trees planted in between to keep them steady. A man's place. Hard to climb, especially with a baby and a small boy who danced eagerly from one stone to the next. But finally, I was there. Between two huge rocks, which had seemed small from below, almost ready to fall down. Not now, not from where I stood, carefully balancing myself on two hard flat stones. My brother looked back at me, then dodged away and disappeared.

I followed, worried that I would lose him. His legs still moved too quickly for me. Then I saw it. A small opening in the rocks, so carefully hidden by branches that if my brother's hand had not been there, waving, I would have missed it. Surely the enemy would have missed it too, I thought, and then my heart beat fast, as I knew I would find a dangerous secret.

Until then, I had never faced danger, not like that. Snakes in the fields, a crocodile down at the river when it was swollen with rain, a nail which had bitten deep into my foot — these were the only kinds of danger that I had met. But this time, it would be different. I had heard too much in the sleeping hut at night, not to know. Our men were fighting the enemy, the people in Salisbury who were oppressing us. They were the ones who had taken away my father and beaten him one night. He was now in prison. With other men, from other villages. Detained, just because he had attended a meeting.

It was dark behind the rocks, but enough light came in for me to see the cave, the low walls, a small fire, two men sitting, and another lying down. One of the men tried to stand up, but because the rock was low, he had to keep his back bent. 'Little sister, we need help,' he said. 'We need food tonight, we cannot move. Our comrade has been hurt by the enemy.'

Did he say all that at once? I remember only the message, the words themselves are no longer so clear. But that face, oh, how I remember that face. Like a young boy fresh from school, clean, huge brown eyes. And a way of speaking that the young men in our village did not use.

I know that that was when I fell in love. When he spoke to me. Looked at me. Even though I knew I might never see him again. His name, his Chimurenga name of course, was Fearless. He told me once more what they needed. Clean water, clean clothes, food. I nodded, too shy to speak. I no longer noticed what my brother was doing, hardly felt Chisi on my back. I saw only Fearless.

When it was dark, I returned. My mother was worried, but she knew I had to go. I had promised that we would tell no one, no one at all. My brother, too, had promised. He had been seen by Fearless when he had climbed the rocks to fetch a goat which had strayed. We went together, my brother and I, to meet them and bring food. He asked me if I went to school, how old I was, if I knew already if I would marry. I was 14 and because my father was in detention, I no longer went to school. There was no money.

So that is how it began. I went to the rocks six times, every night, with my small brother. Every time, I brought food and water. Every time, we talked. He came from a place near the border, and had been operating in our area for some weeks when his comrade was hurt. We talked and I learnt so much. About the regime, about the war, about the comrades and camps, far away in other countries, in Zambia and Mozambique.

All day, I thought of Fearless. I knew the names of the other two comrades, but they had no life for me. Only Fearless and my love for him. Did he love me? I think that, yes, there *was* something. But we never spoke of such things.

When I climbed up again on the seventh day, my brother said, 'They have gone.' I stopped and looked. Yes, he was right. The small opening in the rocks was sealed, as if there had never been anyone. Slowly I bent down, sank on my knees, and carefully took away some of the trees. But it was so — the place was empty. Nothing was left, not even a stone where the fire had been.

I cried when we went back to the village. My brother said nothing and my mother asked nothing. I was miserable, more than I have ever been before or since that night.

The next day, I told my mother that I had to go far to fetch wood, because there were few places nearby where I could find some. She agreed, knowing that what I had said was true. I had not spent any time gathering wood for seven days. So I went, because I wanted to be alone. I knew the others suspected something, but I wanted to think about Fearless and our talks and my love.

I came back late, with a big load on my head. When I passed the cattle enclosure which belonged to my uncle, I knew there was something wrong. The fence was torn down and there were bricks on the path. My mother's house was empty. Things were thrown around. Pots were broken. I ran to the other huts. All empty. I was afraid and ran into the bush, but not to the place where I had met the comrades — that would be dangerous.

In another place, a shelter which the girls had built to keep the small children out of the sun when we worked in the fields, I found two older girls, Gladys and Winnie, hiding under big branches of trees. Like me, they had been out looking for wood. They had come back earlier and seen people being put into lorries. 'The régime came,' they said. 'They took everyone. Your mother also and yes, your brother and Chisi. All of them. They burnt some huts and they chased the cattle. We hid.'

So that was how it was. Later, I discovered that the soldiers had taken the people to what they called a 'keep', a 'protected village' and they could come back and look after the fields, if they could walk there. It was far, that place, and hard for my mother, without me to help.

She told me this and other things when I returned long after the struggle. But that night, I and the other girls walked into the bush and did what I had known I wanted to do, soon after I had met the comrades — join the war and find Fearless.

I did join the struggle and I became a commander. But I never found Fearless. Nor did I ever forget him.

Caroline

I come from Mtoko. Life was very hard there. I was 15 years old when I joined the struggle, while I was at Nyamuzuwe, a Methodist boarding school. I had been there for about one and a half years when the first freedom fighters came to the school. We knew there was a war. The Smith forces came and told us there were 'terrorists' in the area. At first, the freedom fighters came only once or twice a month. Some of our relatives were in hot soup at that time, because the Smith forces had told them to report the presence of 'terrorists'. Some people were killed because the comrades thought that they were traitors and had informed on them.

Then the teachers, almost all of them, were taken away to gaol. We did no schoolwork in those days. At night, the freedom fighters came to teach us about the war and our oppression, and we stayed up until the dawn, singing and talking with them. This meant that we slept during the day. Then one day in 1977, the comrades came and closed the school. They took the fittest, about 15 of us. We were not trained, of course, and when we heard firing during the night, some people ran and were shot. I think that about five or six children died that night. We had to leave them, since we could not take or bury them.

Altogether, we walked for three days. When we finally crossed the border into Mozambique, FRELIMO comrades looked after us and gave us food and clothes. Then we walked about 120 km to a camp called Mororo, in Tete. That is where I stayed until December 1979. Before we went to a camp for training, we had to undergo interrogation. There were always Smith informers, some of whom brought in poison which they had been given, to kill the comrades.

Life was hard for the women. Most women comrades, like myself, were political commissars. I could have done nursing, but I did not like that, so I became a political commissar. Women were not given the same chances as men to train outside the country, so I spent the war period in Mozambique. I was in battles. Once, there was an air raid — a bomb attack. That was in November 1977. We had been in the houses in the commando areas, cleaning the houses of commanders. When we first heard the planes, we thought they were Mozambican planes. Then the bombs dropped. Many people in that camp were not trained and they ran instead of taking cover. Most of them were killed. It was a transit camp, a place from where people were sent elsewhere.

I was wearing a red dress, so I took it off and covered myself with leaves, and crawled away. I was very lucky. My sister was in the kitchen at the time and it was the kitchen which was attacked first. She was injured in the leg, but managed to escape. My brother, who was also in the camp, had bomb fragments all over his body.

Many women attended courses after the war and, as exercises, wrote down their experiences. Some of these were published in *Young Women in the Liberation Struggle: Stories and Poems from Zimbabwe.*[3]

Footnotes:

1. 'Chimurenga' is the term used for the armed struggles of the late 1890s and the 1970s.

2. A woman has since been appointed to sit on the Public Service Commission.

3. Kathy Bond-Stewart (ed): (Harare: Zimbabwe Publishing House) 1984.

Ancestral Spirit

Guard over them, Lord
Ancestral Spirit
Guard over them, Lord.

Grandmother Nehanda
Our ancestral spirit
Grandmother Nehanda
Our ancestral spirit
Look after us, Lord
So we may return
to Zimbabwe
Today people are suffering
Our mothers are suffering
Our fathers are suffering
When shall we repossess Zimbabwe?
Ancestral spirit
Ancestral spirit
Guard over us

2

THE FIRST CHIMURENGA

The Parliament of Zimbabwe is at the centre of the nation's capital, Harare. The visitor is instantly struck by the colonial atmosphere, as well as by the formalities reminiscent of Westminster, the 'mother' of Parliament. There are two Chambers, a Speaker's Chair (a recent gift by Britain), and a gallery that was once hung with the portraits of British kings and queens. Some British-type cartoons remain in the Members' lounge and the corridors are still partly decorated with the mementoes of 90 years of colonial rule.

But on the imposing staircase which sweeps down from the ministerial and other offices on the first floor, there stands a figure that is wholly Zimbabwean. Its subject is a woman, an African woman. Her features are strong, unsmiling and confident. Strangers, naturally, ask who she is; but Zimbabweans know. She is Mbuya Nehanda — heroine, ancestor, spirit-medium. It is fitting that she should stand guard in this place as a symbol of the new Zimbabwe, for she played a significant role in the struggle to build it. In many ways, she is also the symbol of the African women who, like her, suffered in the name of freedom.

Zimbabwe is inhabited by 180,000 Whites, some seven and a half million Africans, 10,000 people of mixed race and 23,000 Asians. Of the Africans, 80% belong to the Shona-speaking people; about 15% are Ndebele; and the rest are a mixture of other peoples, such as the Tonga and Shangaan.

The Shona (a name in general use only since the last century) are the oldest inhabitants of the region. Their history began with the people of the early and late Iron Age, who moved into the area and, it seems, displaced the Stone Age people (from whom the Khoisan, who live in Namibia and Botswana, are descended). The historian David Beach has traced the rise and fall of the Shona dynasties and clans who lived, fought and roamed in what is now Zimbabwe and Mozambique.[1] Thanks to their advanced tools, he writes, the Iron Age people were able to build huts and to plough the land. They also knew how to mine and work iron and gold ore. Beach fixes the earliest known Iron Age settlement at around 180 AD, pointing out that people lived and moved in small family groups. There was thus no single 'founder family' of the Shona people. There were, however, some well-known and powerful families, which organised the creation of several important states. Information about these states has been drawn both from oral history and from the records of the Portuguese, who arrived around 1500, having displaced the Arab traders at Sofala along the eastern coastline. The dynasties of the Changamire (which is colloquially known as the

Mutapa Empire) found their way into European records. The titles of both the Changamire-Razvi dynasty, which subsequently ruled over the Karanga people, was based in the south-west of the country. In their history book for schools, Seidman, Martin and Johnson state that: 'Early in the fifteenth century a man called Mutota moved north to the Zambezi Valley. Some oral traditions say he came from Great Zimbabwe.[2] He settled in the Dande area, ruling over the Tonga and Tavara people...[and] his son Matope became the first Munhumutapa, the ruler of Munhumutapa...The people of the Munhumutapa empire lived in the region between the Tsatse, Mazowe and Zambezi rivers.'[3]

In African religion, which ascribes great powers to the ancestors, history and belief is intertwined — the ancestors are part of life as they are of death. It is the duty of the spirits of the ancestors to ensure the wellbeing of their descendants. The spirit world has as strict a hierarchy as that of the living. No spirit can occupy a higher place in death than she or he had occupied in life. Thus a *mhondoro* is a spirit of the founder of a clan and a *mudzimu* is the spirit of the father or grandfather of a living person. The spirits which Beach has described as super-*mhondoro* are national spirits, recognised by, and responsible for, all the people. Mbuya Nehanda is one such super-*mhondoro*.

The Zimbabwean writer Aeneas Chingwedere believes that an ancestor family of the Shona arrived some thousand years ago, between 1000 to 1050 AD, from Tanganyika. These took possession of the land controlled by the previous occupants, the Hungwe, whom they defeated and absorbed to form a new and vigorous nation. The founder of the dynasty, he states, was Murenga Sororenzou, whose children included Chaminuka, the greatest of the super-*mhondoro*, Runji, Mushavutu and Nehanda.[4] He recounts that Nehanda had died before the family actually reached the Zambezi and that her spirit had taken possession of a medium — a n'anga. This person took up a wooden rod, 'whereupon the waters parted and the family crossed'.

To understand the history of the people, one has to understand something of their beliefs and culture. The Mwari cult is part of this intricate pattern of beliefs. Mwari is God, 'He-who-has-no-human-form'. His presence is everywhere: he speaks from rocks and trees. As it is customary that great men are given praise names, so Mwari, too, has other names. He also has several High Places, such as Great Zimbabwe and the Matopos. As it is also customary never to address an important person directly, it is unacceptable to address Mwari directly. it must be done through the *mhondoro*, the *vadzimu*, and of course the national spirits, the super-*mhondoro* such as Chaminuka or Nehanda. High priests, who served Mwari, were part of the Mwari cult. Historians have yet to agree on the reasons why Chaminuka, Nehanda and Kaguvi assumed such a great importance during the last century. What *is* known, is that the spirit mediums of both Nehanda and Kaguvi played a

Great Zimbabwe

decisive role at the time of the coming of the White man in 1890. The best-known spirit medium of Chaminuka was killed earlier in the nineteenth century.

The arrival of the so-called 'Pioneer Column' — 200 men of assorted skills, accompanied by 500 policemen, all servants of the British South African Company (BSAC) that had been founded by Cecil John Rhodes — was a straightforward act of aggression against the peoples of both Mashonaland and Matabeleland. On a plaque that is still visible in the centre of Harare, it is written that on 12 September, 1890, Mashonaland was occupied by the 'first civilian population of Mashonaland'. No mention is made of the already existing 'civilian population', the Shona people. Evidently, no one in the Pioneer Column had any notion of the intricate pattern of Shona society.

In fact, the Shona had developed a system which enabled them to organise major states and to build one of the greatest of all pre-colonial African towns — Great Zimbabwe. Zimbabwe means 'house of stone': today, it is the name of the young country which, until 1980, was named after Cecil Rhodes. Great Zimbabwe has been dated by archaeologists at around the year 1200. Until Independence, the site near Masvingo in the south-west of the country was labelled as the 'Zimbabwe Ruins' and was 'sold' to tourists as a 'great mystery'. Tourist pamphlets suggested that the site must have been developed by Europeans — even though the archaeologist Peter Garlake had produced evidence that the indigenous peoples must have been its architects.

Peter Garlake has describe the pattern of life in the ancient town, which housed thousands of people with their cattle, their hunting gear, their pottery and their skills.[5] Great Zimbabwe was also the palace of the king, a shrine to Mwari and a market place. Its great walls were built not for defence, but as a sign of prosperity and power. Garlake writes that:

The wall around the Great Enclosure is over 250 metres long and uses 15,000 tonnes of stone blocks. The skills of the masons is very striking. The style of the architecture is unique. Bringing men together on such a scale is an impressive administrative and social achievement. The population of Great Zimbabwe, well over 10,000 people, made it the largest city of Black Africa in its time.

By about 1500, however, Great Zimbabwe had become deserted and the gold and copper mines and the iron smelting works no longer functioned. The reasons for this have yet to be fully established, but the most credible theory is that the inhabitants of Great Zimbabwe, who relied heavily on cattle, exhausted the land resources in the area and were forced to seek new pastures.

A German explorer, Carl Mauch, was the first European to stumble upon Great Zimbabwe, in the 1870s. Its existence had already been known in Europe through the descriptions of its glory by the Portuguese geographer Joau de Barros, who based his information on second-hand reports. Other Europeans who came after Mauch took away some of Great Zimbabwe's treasures, including the stone birds that had sat on huge pillars. Only in 1980, after Independence, were five of them returned to their rightful home. The Zimbabwe bird has become the symbol of the new country.

The Portuguese traders and travellers made much of the fabled Mutapa Empire. The label 'empire', writes David Beach, probably stems from this source. It appears to have been a characteristic of the Shona people to create state structures, some of which were strong enough to exact tribute from other, smaller, states. The power struggles between different groups and states, as well as within states, by followers of different leaders, mirror similar events in every corner of the globe. What clearly emerges is that the Mutapa and Changamire dynasties were very powerful and were able to raise armies of fighting men. There is no doubt that the rulers of the time were wealthy and revered and their courts lavish. The wealth was partly derived from trade in gold and other commodities, but the base of power was cattle.

The Shona people appear to identify with a region and a place. As their field of activities ranged right down to the coastal area, it is clear that the borders which divide the coastal people from those on the high plateau were generally a colonial convention, unknown before 1820. There is thus no single history of the Shona, but a web of regional histories. What unifies them is a common language and culture and, in specific cases, a common national spirit. The might of the Mutapa Empire was broken down by the arrival of the Portuguese, who not only settled in the coastal region and took over trade from the Arabs, but also created the *prazo*-system (the farming of large tracts of land). In time, it was difficult to distinguish the *prazo* owners from the African rulers. Some Shona chiefs became vassals of the Portuguese and others were defeated, as the newcomers played one group off against another in their search for concessions and trade. Despite these interventions, the Mutapa Empire survived until 1884, thus spanning a period of five centuries. In 1884, however, the Portuguese renewed their interest in the area. They made war on the Mutapa and installed rulers of their own choice, who were forced to pay tribute. This division of the Mutapa Empire might have continued if the British had not succeeded the Portuguese and created a new national unit: Southern Rhodesia.

The so called Berlin Conference of 1884 formulated the ground rules of a game which became known as 'the Scramble for Africa'. Africa had become the subject of exploration during the early part of the century. Once Henry Morton Stanley, the journalist-explorer who (curiously) became famous for his four words, 'Dr Livingstone, I presume,' had solved the mystery of the Congo River for Europeans, a new phase began. Missionaries had already visited and settled in various African states before 1884. Traders too, following in the footsteps of the Portuguese and Dutch (who settled at the Cape in 1652), had come into contact with the African people.

In the last quarter of the century, however, new forces were at work in Europe. Germany and Italy became unified. The Belgian King, Leopold II, was anxious to acquire wealth and power through a colonial empire. The new factories of Europe suffered a recession at around the same time and the search for new markets, as well as for secure sources of raw materials, began. As a result, the European powers came into conflict with each other. Eventually, the German Chancellor, with the French as partners, convened a colonial conference in Berlin. For 13 weeks, the Europeans attempted to settle the future of Africa. Afterwards, they competed fiercely with each other for African territory and began to define colonial borders. Africa still lives with these same borders.

In the south, a bitter conflict ensued between the British, who had taken over the Cape from the Dutch in 1797, and the Boers, descendants of the Dutch, who resented British rule and had moved into the interior, establishing their own republics. There was conflict, too, between the British and the Germans. In 1884, the Germans occupied the territory that is now known as Namibia — this occupation was a major reason for the Berlin Conference.

Cecil Rhodes — imperialist, Cape politician and financier — was determined to establish British rule all the way from the Cape to Cairo. To this end, he began the construction of a railway that stretched north from the Cape to the borders of Zaire (as it is known today). He also formed the British South Africa Company (BSAC), which succeeded in obtaining a royal charter. This company, known as Charter, sent its messengers into the interior and obtained concessions from African kings, who little suspected that they were signing their heritage away. Two such kings were Lobengula, head of the Ndebele, and Litunga, head of the Lozi people in Barotseland (today the Western Province of Zambia).

With these concessions, Rhodes and his men felt themselves to be legally justified in occupying the territory that became Southern Rhodesia (Zimbabwe) and Northern Rhodesia (Zambia), across the Zambezi. Despite resistance and actual wars in the 1890s, company rule was successfully established. The two territories became BSAC property and were administered by BSAC officials. Although the Company relinquished direct possession in 1922, the BSAC insignia were worn by the police force in Rhodesia until the day of Independence in 1980. But today, the so-called BSAP has become the ZRP (Zimbabwe Republic Police).

Even before the arrival of the Pioneer Column, the Shona had been forced to accommodate strangers. These were the Ndebele, who settled in the southern part of the country under the king, Mzilikazi. The Ndebele migration had been caused by the *mfecane*, the terrible period of unrest and movement that was triggered off by the wars of Shaka, the warrior king of the Zulus. Mzilikazi, himself a Ngoni, who wished to escape Shaka, moved north, first settling in what is now the Transvaal Province of South Africa. On his way, he was joined by other people fleeing from Shaka. Defeated by the Boers in battle, he crossed the Limpopo river in 1839 into what was the Changamire region. This sealed the Changamire's fate. Defeated, a number of chiefs acknowledged the Ndebele king as their ruler. In the decade of 1840-50, Ndebele power was firmly established in what became Matabeleland. Mzilikazi did not have to deal with the Whites, though he did welcome some missionaries into his area. It was his son, King Lobengula, who was confronted with the problem. In 1888, representatives of the BSAC succeeded in obtaining a concession from him which granted the BSAC a monopoly 'over all metals and minerals situated and contained in my kingdoms.' The kingdoms were named as Matabeleland and Mashonaland.

The arrival of the Pioneer Column — described as an *impi* by Lobengula — greatly alarmed him. But worse was to come. The Whites were disappointed to find that the geological structure of Zimbabwe was not similar to that of South Africa's Golden Reef, as they had expected. Today there are about 150 small goldmines, but neither in size nor output can they be compared with the South African mines. Nor were there any diamonds (though Zimbabwe does have other treasures: emeralds, semi-precious stones and many base minerals such as asbestos, nickel, copper and chrome). In their quest for profit, the BSAC finally resorted to land — if there was no mineral wealth, at least there was good arable soil. They obtained concessions that allowed them to establish huge farms in the most fertile regions. The company either gave the land to settlers or sold it for very low prices. The Africans who had been displaced were forced onto the less productive land in the outer regions.

Lobengula, gravely disturbed by the activities of the Europeans, attempted to regain control. As an initial concession, he had been granted a monthly retainer of £100 during his lifetime, as well as 1,000 rifles, ammunition and the promise of a boat (later converted to cash). Regretting the bargain, he repudiated the concession — but without success.

Three years after the coming of the Whites, the Ndebele, assisted by the Mwari High Priests, rose in — as it is known in European history books — the 'Matabele Rebellion'. It was a hopeless undertaking from the Ndebele point of view. The Ndebele armoury was useless against the BSAC Maxim guns. Lobengula was defeated and Matabeleland occupied. In 1896, another attempt was made, together with the people of Mashonaland. This time, the Ndebele were routed, their regiments broken up and more of their land was lost to the White invaders. But to the dismay of the Whites, this was not the end of the fighting. They had underestimated the Shona and misunderstood their nature and society. Little was known of their history, their proud record, the states and the dynasties that had reigned so long and so successfully. A story is told of a BSAC official who wrote a letter home telling how the 'natives' had finally become pacified. But ironically, this letter was written when the author's death had already been predestined. In his 'compound' sat a messenger who had been despatched by Mbuya Nehanda. The spirit medium had spoken and her messengers were travelling from village to village: the people were to rise up and kill the White men. Neither the letter-writer, Rhodes, nor the BSAC shareholders in London, knew of the importance of Mbuya Nehanda.

In 1896, the Nehanda spirit medium, a woman by the name of Charwe, lived in the Shamva Valley, through which the Mazowe river passes on its way to become a tributary of the Zambezi. Nehanda's message was unambiguous: the ancestors wished the people to take up arms and fight. She promised no success, however. The war would be lost, she said, and she herself would die. Nonetheless, the command of the ancestors had to be obeyed. It is believed that she herself led her people into battle, just like Kaguvi, another famous spirit medium.

A Jesuit, Fr. A. Boos, wrote about this event:

In the case of the Mashonas the incredible happened. This degraded, cowardly race, which for so many years had proved an easy prey to the Matabele raiders, at whose approach they would flee to their mountain fortress without thought of resistance, actually dared, at the bidding of their prophets, to engage in a war of extermination with the White colonists; and though defeated again and again, they continued to offer a stubborn resistance from their rocky strongholds, buoyed up with their unwavering belief in the promises of the witch-doctors.[6]

Mbuya Nehanda and Sekuru Kaguvi were the most important of these 'prophets'. Nehanda's prophecy came true: the Shona were defeated, and she and Kaguvi were captured, tried and sentenced to death by hanging. Another Jesuit, Fr. Francis Richartz, gave an account of the execution:

to Neanda I did not speak until evening, in order to avoid a scene, though I had a long quiet talk with her, which made me feel even hopeful.

Mbuya Nehanda (c.1862-1898). A powerful woman spirit medium who was committed to upholding traditional Shona culture, Mbuya Nehanda helped to organise nationwide resistance to colonial rule during the Chimurenga of 1896-97. This inspired leader was captured and after trial sentenced to death in Salisbury.

However, when in the evening about 6 o'clock I saw her again and in the presence of Victor, who tried his best to persuade her to listen to me, I told her that she had to die next morning, she began to behave like a mad woman. She took her blankets and wished to leave the cell, and when told to remain and keep quiet, she refused and said she never would endure to be locked up. When I saw that nothing could be done with her I went away with Victor and Neanda began to dance, to laugh and talk, so that the warders were obliged to tie her hands and watch her continually, as she threatened to kill herself.

On Wednesday April 27th I again made an attempt to speak to Neanda and bring her to a better frame of mind, but she refused, called for her people and wanted to go back to her own country, the Mazoe — and die there, and behaved as she had done the night before. When I saw that nothing could be done with her, the time for execution having arrived, I left Neanda and went to Kakubi who received me in good disposition. Whilst I was conversing with him, Neanda was taken out to the scaffold. Her cries and resistance when she was taken up the ladder, the screaming and yelling on the scaffold disturbed my conversation with Kakubi very much, until the noisy opening of the trap-door upon which she stood followed by the heavy thud of her body as it fell, made an end to the interruption.[7]

Today Zimbabweans are proud of the fact that Nehanda refused to submit, resisting conversion and persuasion to the last. The period of 1896-97 is known by the Shona as The First Chimurenga, the first war of resistance.

In what became Southern Rhodesia, tax systems, a well known tool to force Africans into cash employment, were introduced. Then, in 1930, the Land Apportionment Act was used legally to divide the country into racial categories. These were as follows:

	Per Cent
Tribal Trust Land (African land held according to custom)	*41.6*
African Purchase Land (individual holdings of African — male — farmers)	*4.4*
European area (White farms plus all urban areas)	*37.0*
National Land (Forest Reserves, National Parks)	*10.9*

In 1969, the Land Tenure Act replaced the 1930 legislation, giving a little more land to Africans, at the expense of unreserved and national land.

The division of land into Black and White ownership was patently unfair, not only because the land had originally belonged to the Africans, but also because of the discrepancy in population statistics: in 1900 there were only some 11,000 Whites and this had increased to a mere 270,000 by 1972. Africans numbered 700,000 in 1900 and by the 1970s, had increased to almost seven million. When the rule of the BSAC ended, the Whites were granted self-rule. They elected their own legislature with the British Government, which was represented by a ceremonial governor. Africans became a class of poor peasants and workers, displaced from their own land. The fabric of their society changed dramatically and so, too, did the status of African women.

The Second Chimurenga is the war which ended in December 1979 with the signing of the Lancaster House agreement in London. The conference was held under the auspices of the British colonial power, which had invited to the negotiation table the contesting parties: Ian Smith and Bishop Abel Muzorewa on the one hand, and the Patriotic Front, composed of the two liberation movements (ZAPU under Joshua Nkomo and ZANU under Robert Mugabe), on the other. The conference was brought about by the 'hot phase' of the Second Chimurenga, the successful period of the long and drawn-out conflict with the White settlers which began in the sixties and 'hotted up' in the north-eastern region in 1972.

As in 1896, a Nehanda spirit medium played a major role in the struggle for freedom. At this time, the Nehanda medium was an aged lady, well over 80 years old, who lived in the Msengezi district. When the first trained ZANU guerrillas entered the border villages, they asked the villagers for help. As the colonial economy had drawn most of the young men away from the rural areas, they were mainly populated by women (80 per cent of all women in Zimbabwe live in the rural areas), children and the old. The women consulted the spirit medium. Mbuya Nehanda's response was instant and clear: the time had come for the land of the ancestors to be wrested from the Whites. The people must fight. This time, she said, they would be successful.

When the first shots were fired in this region, the Smith régime mistook them for a renewed incursion from across the Zambezi, such as had occurred in the sixties. Once the error had been realised and 'good old Smithy' began to mutter about those 'witchdoctors' who led the people astray, it was too late. The signal for the support of the *vakomana* (our boys) had been given and was being fully obeyed: the freedom fighters were offered full protection and were integrated into the fabric of traditional society.

Martin and Johnson give the following account of the old lady who was Nehanda's medium:

Urimbo, who was directing guerilla operations from a Frelimo base, remembers Mbuya Nehanda as a small woman, very thin and very old, with white hair and skin which was exceedingly black.

She was dressed in a piece of black cloth that was wrapped around her body and she wore bangles, some of them gold, on her wrists, and other ornaments around her body. Her skin was dry and cracked with age, and gum was regularly rubbed on to protect it from the sun.[8]

Subsequently, Mbuya was carried out of the country for her protection, to a camp (Chifombo) in Zambia. She died there a year later, having completed her task.

It was thus a woman who initiated the war in village society and it was women, the rural women, who carried the burden of this guerrilla war. From hiding and feeding the young men, they progressed to carrying messages and, finally, to joining them in active struggle. Ironically, it was the changes wrought by colonialism in the pattern of African society, thereby changing the composition of the rural population, which paved the way for the full participation of women: first in the political unrest of the fifties, and later, in the bushwar which raged from 1972 until 1979.

Footnotes:

1. D.N. Beach: *The Shona and Zimbabwe, 900-1850: An outline of Shona History* (Gweru: Mambo Press) 1980.

2. Great Zimbabwe, the site of a major African town from which Modern Zimbabwe derives its name, was built over a period of 200 years from about 1200AD. Formerly known as the 'Zimbabwe Ruins', the majestic walls and courtyards have intrigued tourists over decades. Other smaller 'Zimbabwes' exist on several sites in the country. The word Zimbabwe means 'a house built of stone'.

3. Seidman, Martin and Johnson: *A New History of Zimbabwe* (Harare: Zimbabwe Publishing House) 1982, p.24.

4. Chingwedere's writings include: *From Mutapa to Rhodes* (London: Macmillan) 1980 and *Lobola: the pros and cons* (Harare: Books for Africa) 1982. The first book has aroused controversy over the purported origins of the Shona. However, no historian has so far been able to establish precisely where the Shona-speaking people came from.

5. Peter Garlake, *Great Zimbabwe Described and Explained* (Harare: Zimbabwe Publishing House) 1982.

6. 'Extracts from Zambezi Mission Records', *Moto* (Harare), June 1982.

7. As 6. Neanda and Kukubi are the spellings used in mission records instead of 'Nehanda' and 'Kaguvi' as spelt by the Shona.

8. D. Martins and P. Johnson: *The Struggle for Zimbabwe* (Harare: Zimbabwe Publishing house) 1981, p.75.

3

DIFFERENT REALITIES: BLACK 'COLOURED', AND WHITE WOMEN

Black Women in the Rural Areas

In order to run the mines and then, when the commercial emphasis was shifted to the land, to run the farms, the Whites required a large labour force. As administrative posts and market towns became established, additional labourers were required to service the White households as domestic servants. It was nearly always male labourers that were wanted. The White man's perception of African women was even lower than the one he had of his own women: he saw them as purchased chattel living in a backward society.

The mechanisms of drawing the African male into the White man's cash economy were several: by driving Africans onto impoverished land, which became overcrowded and increasingly less productive, men were forced to look for paid work. The establishment of taxes, which presupposed the possession of cash, created a further need for wages. And in those cases where it was difficult to attract labour — particularly at the mines — forced labour was introduced. But with low wages and the denial of any social benefits, such as a pension and provisions for sickness and unemployment, the land still remained the sole source of security for these men.

Only the boys were eligible to attend the mission schools. These schools taught the basic skills required by White employers: a smattering of English and some familiarity with the customs of the settler minority. While the men were away, the women, the old people and the children, had to do the jobs which had previously been done by men, who rarely returned to the village. It was a mixed blessing. On the one hand, women lost much of their self-respect. As the White man's civilisation began to be seen as desirable, women put less value on their vital role within traditional society. And, as few women were being educated in the White man's ways, they came to feel inferior to the men who had gone to school and moved in the world of the Whites.

But on the other hand, women were not so contaminated as men by foreign ideas. Even in the later stages of colonialism, the rural women (who remained the majority of African women) were largely cut off from foreign influence, even from Christianity. Where women did become Christians, due to the wide network of missions of various denominations (which did, in fact, serve a useful purpose by providing health and educational services), the woman wove the new beliefs into those of the old.

Most important of all, however, was the fact that women became more self-reliant. As some of the freedom fighters of later generations said, 'anything a man can do, we can do.' The woman, left to fend by herself for the family and the land, took on the roles that had previously been the preserve of the male. Ironically, it was the hand of colonialism that prepared her for the vital role she played in the Second Chimurenga of the 1970s.

Caroline Katsande

Life in pre-independent Zimbabwe, according to the young Caroline Katsande, was very difficult for a woman on her own.

> We were very poor. My father had died when I was very young. I was the last born of one brother and three sisters. We had a field, but my mother could not work on the land — she had to earn cash, so she worked for other people, for money. Whenever anyone needed some help, my mother would go and work. She needed money for our school fees. I first started to plough when I was 10 years old. In those days, there was something called 'bottleneck screening', which meant that not everyone could be educated. I went to school, but I had little time because I also worked as a nanny for other people. My mother would get up at 3 a.m., cook our breakfast, and then go out to work all day. Food was mainly mealie cobs, which we ate during the day. Tea was only something we had on special occasions, when visitors came with sugar and bread. My clothes were second-hand, passed on to me by relatives who lived nearby. When their children could no longer wear the dresses which had become too small for them, then they were given to me. I used to walk one kilometre each day to a primary school run by Methodists. I was bright and did well in grade 7, so my brother paid for me to go to secondary school.

The theme of hard, back-grinding work runs through *We Carry A Heavy Load*[1] and a report issued by the Ministry of Community Development and Women's Affairs in 1982. The latter provides the following description of a day in the life of a rural woman (described in official statistics as 'economically inactive'):

4.30 a.m.-6.00 a.m.	*—Get up, go and fetch water,*
	—Prepare breakfast for school children,
	—Eat sadza or drink tea, leave for field.
6.00a.m.-11.00a.m.	*—Work in the field,*

	—*Short break,* —*Back to work,* —*occasionally attending to the cattle.*
2.30 pm - 3.00 pm	—*Lunch prepared on site or brought from home if anybody else is available.*
3.00 pm - 6.30 pm	—*Work in the field until it is too dark to see,* —*Collect water or firewood on the way home.*
7.00 pm - 9.00 pm	—*Grind some rapoko,* —*Cook with inadequate wood,* —*Bath self and children, if water and energy are still available.*

Given this pattern of life, broken only by a beer festival or an important occasion such as a wedding or a funeral, it is understandable that women had no trouble in understanding that they were oppressed.

When the Land Husbandry Act was passed in order to stop overcrowding in the TTLs (Tribal Trust Lands) by culling the cattle, it was the women on the land who were affected — and it was they who rebelled. Deprived of their husbands, forced to take over the man's work as well as their own, rural women needed no one to tell them they were living in an unjust society.

Sekai

Sekai Makwavarara looked frail. But as she moved to fetch mats for her visitors, it was clear that the first impression was deceptive: she was thin, yes, but she was also wiry. Her back was unbent, her legs unmarked by age. Only her wrinkled face and arms and some missing teeth indicated her age. Her hair was hidden beneath a piece of cloth, the *doek* worn by so many rural African women. 'My mother is almost 80,' her son said. 'I know, because I myself am 48. Her lastborn.' He translated patiently, as patiently as she answered the questions. Only once he volunteered something on his own when we walked through the fields, for which purpose he drew on a pair of sturdy gumboots — 'From South Africa.' He, like his father before him, had worked in a South African goldmine.

'I was alone for many years. No, no money came. When he returned, there was money for a while. But he was sick.'

The old lady spoke softly, quickly. She explained that two children had died while her husband had been away, two girls. Two sons had survived.

I came here when I married. They paid many cattle for me. I was young and strong. I had two sons quickly. Then the girls. My husband left when the fourth girl was born. His mother fell ill then. She was bewitched. No n'anga could do anything. She died while he was away. He sent money for that.

The village, nestling against a group of granite rocks, was a good half hour's walk from the fields. But Mrs Makwavarara had planted vegetables near her kitchen hut.

The children's sleeping hut was there once. A long time ago. We have water here. It is a good place.

Tomatoes, rape, cabbages, all well-watered and well-cared for.

I still go to the field every day. I have my own cattle and some goats too.

She disappeared, returning with a huge, beautiful pot.

I made that.

What was her life like, when the children had been small and her husband was away? 'No different. I learnt many things.' She rose to fetch a wooden container, carefully carved, and her cooking utensils, and then began to grind a handful of corn, moving rhythmically, to show what she meant.

In the morning, the small children came with me to the fields. Before I left, I prepared food for the old people. I returned when it became very hot. Stamped mealies for sadza. Brought back wood, if I could; otherwise, if one of the children was sick or I had to carry other things or water, I had to go out again to fetch wood. Then I cooked, fed the people, ate, then I slept.

Was this her life, every day?

Every day. Of course work changed, when the rains came or in the dry weather. There were also many feasts. Burials. Marriages. Many things. One year the drought had been terrible. All the people had been told to come together, so that we could go there . .

She pointed towards a mountain, whose curious shape, pearlike and flat-topped, gave it the appearance of a half-peeled fruit.

We all walked there to pray. The chief and the n'angas were there. We had brewed beer, sweet beer. Everyone drank, yes, also the children, and we danced, danced all day and all night. Beer was brought also to the caves.

For the ancestors — though she did not say so and we did not press her.

The rains came very late that year and we had to go to the bush to look for fruits and grasses. It was a bad year. That was the last time the children died.

She talked without emotion, her eyes dimmed with age. No, she had not been to school. Yes, she was a Christian, she had gone to Church at a mission nearby, when she was young. Not any more. Her sons had gone to the mission school. And the war? She shook her head. Yes, there had been suffering. But no, the war was something else. Something she did not want to talk about.

She rose to make us tea. 'It's the first time she had ever had a White visitor,' said her son. 'This is a TTL. No Whites came, except the District Commissioner.'

Black Women in the Town

A single woman is not entitled to municipal housing even if she has children. She is legally a minor, whatever her age, and cannot enter into a contract or lease. There is no question here of the guardian's permission: it is against the present housing policy...

From *The Woman's Guide to Law Through Life*, University of Rhodesia, 1979.

Esther

The 20% of women who did go to town, usually stayed with their husbands or in a 'location'. Some women drifted into prostitution or, if they were lucky, into independent work as market women. It was rare in Southern Rhodesia to employ a 'girl'; 'boys' (these labels were used whatever the age of the men or women employed) were preferred. One exception was Esther. She was a young woman who became a client of advocate Jan McGrowther, who had come to Rhodesia in the sixties to practise as the country's only woman advocate. Jan had been asked to act for the defence at criminal sessions in Bulawayo in a number of homicide cases. In her view, the inadequate time and briefing of the defence clearly reflected the values of society — that it 'didn't matter', as it was 'only Blacks' who had killed each other. The use of a defence counsel was merely compliance with the letter, not the spirit, of the law.

Esther, who had been charged with the murder of her new-born baby, became one of her clients. She had been working in a household in Bulawayo when her pregnancy was discovered and she had been dismissed. She then returned to her village. When it was time for her to have the child, she had walked to a clinic some 20 kilometres away. There, she was assisted only by a midwife; after the birth, she was on her own. In the morning, her baby was born; in the afternoon, she was told to get up and go home. After a while she became tired. Her recorded confession stated that she had 'strangled the baby and hidden it under a bush, then gone home to tell her father that the child was dead. No reason was given for this conduct.' Jan McGrowther decided that this was not 'murder' but 'infanticide' — a term which takes into account the mental disorder that can be provoked by childbirth. But since there was no such offence as infanticide under Rhodesian law, Esther was charged with first degree murder, which carried the death penalty.

Esther was portrayed by the prosecution as a semi-prostitute, conscious of what she had done, whose only desire was to return to the bright lights of Bulawayo. The further claim that she had been afraid of her father, because she was carrying an illegitimate child, exemplified the widespread ignorance of African traditions — for no African child is seen as illegitimate. Jan McGrowther rejected the prosecution's case. When she finally met her client, she saw a young and naive 18 year old, who replied honestly to all her questions. Esther said that she thought she had fallen asleep and remembered looking down on the child and seeing that it was dead. She had been afraid of her father, but only because he wanted the child. Indeed, it was the father who had told the police, which scotched the theory that she had feared her father's anger at an illegitimate birth.

Esther seemed to accept the punishment of death as inevitable. She knew she had killed the child, but could not explain why. To her lawyer, it seemed clear: a young girl, confused after childbirth, sent off alone on a 20 kilometre walk through the bush, hungry and unhappy, had temporarily lost control. Jan McGrowther believed Esther's statement that she had no reason to kill the baby and that her father had deeply mourned the loss of a grandchild.

Jan did her best for Esther, but she could not prevent a tragic outcome. By pleading puerperal mania (temporary insanity) and thereby winning the case, Esther was confined to a mental hospital — even though, at the time of the trial, she was sane. Miss McGrowther had expected the young woman to be released soon. But although she lobbied some White women's groups on Esther's behalf, they were not interested. 'After all, she was only a Black.' It took many years before the law changed and the category of infanticide introduced. 'I do not know when Esther was released,' she said, adding that, 'she was still in this terrible institution when I left Rhodesia.'

Valerie

Valerie thought she was about 50 years old. Once, she said, she had had a husband, but he left her with two children, both girls.

> That made it difficult. In the townships, a woman on her own was considered a prostitute.

This conversation took place in a shop near Harare's Kopje, in what had previously been the red light district. The White woman owner of the shop, which sold second-hand furniture, nodded.

> Come on, Val. Isn't that how you managed too? I remember you buying that huge bed from me....

Valerie, who had refused to sit down on a chair, was kneeling on a mat at our feet. 'That was...so long ago. Who wants me now?' She laughed, unashamed and without apology. 'There was nothing I could do. When I bought that bed, I had already made a little money.' Then she added, a little defensively, 'But I never moved here. I stayed in Highfields.' She added, for my benefit, 'Here I wouldn't have been able to switch — to beer. In the townships, that was easier.'

Beer — that meant a shebeen, an illegal drinking place. Did you have to look after the children? Didn't your husband do anything to help? She seemed indifferent. 'It was difficult. I didn't know where he was. With someone from his village, maybe. I was born here, in town.'

Valerie looked what she was — an energetic, independent woman, who had learnt to fend for herself.

> I made money with the beer. Of course you had to get the police on your side, pay them, give them beer for free. Sometimes they told you they were raiding. Sometimes they didn't.

The shopkeeper explained:

> Valerie is a good customer. She was always buying furniture. Her house became very popular, so she built more rooms. But sometimes she went inside. Prison, I mean!

Valerie grimaced.

> I hated it....Cold showers, early in the morning. They shave your
> hair. The food — oh, it isn't food they give you! Animal food.
> Every time I went inside, I'd swear I'd stop, with the beer and the
> other thing too. But then — you come out and the children are
> hungry and what do you do? You start all over again.

Did she ever want to marry again?

> Oh, men want to marry a shebeen Queen. They know we make
> money. But what would I want to get married for? Men beat you
> when they get drunk. Even if they don't get drunk, they beat you.
> And they only want your money. No, I'll never marry again.
> Sometimes one wants a man. But now I am old. I am glad I am
> alone. My girls are married. No, they're not in the townships now.

She said no more. It didn't seem fair to pry, for survival in the townships
might have lost her the children. And she has been doomed to this, a life
in the twilight of criminality, from which there is no escape. 'She's a
great girl, Valerie,' said the shopkeeper.

> One of the best. When she buys something, I put it away for her, I
> know she'll pay. Doesn't pinch anything, either. I can go out of the
> office and leave money lying around. You can't say that for all of
> them — Valerie's O.K. A real person. Pity there aren't more like
> that.

Rosemary

Esther's attempt to solve her problems failed. Her life outside the
village led to misery and despair, thanks to the White man's laws.
Rosemary, a young woman who became a friend of Mrs Judith Schulz, a
West German living temporarily in Zambia, was more fortunate. After
running away from home, Rosemary married a White man from
Switzerland. She told Mrs Schulz that the marriage was difficult. There
had been problems right from the start. Her father had been furious
when she had told him that she intended to marry a White man.

> He threatened to kill me if I married him. My brother heard him.
> By tradition, it is my brother who is responsible for me. He said
> that it was his place to kill me. My father told him he did not really
> want me dead, he only wanted me to stop thinking of marrying a

White. You see, my father knew of too many mixed marriages in Rhodesia and he knew how many problems they had.

In the two 'Rhodesias', mixed marriages were not forbidden by law. But there was strict segregation and there was a stigma attached to mixed marriages or associations between White and Black. There was also a law forbidding sexual relations between White women and Black men, though White men were free to engage in sexual liaisons with Black women.

Rosemary's mother had died. Her father married again, to a woman who disliked her. She was constantly scolded and beaten. Only her mother's family, her aunt in particular, made any attempt to help her. Born in the urban areas, she grew up with little knowledge of traditional customs and rural life. Her father, anxious to get some money for *lobola*, arranged a marriage very early on and went through the various rituals connected with marrying off a daughter.

The man came from some small village. One morning, his relatives came and tied a goat to a pole near our house. That frightened me. It was all so strange. I told my aunt I did not like the idea of marrying a strange man. So she told me not to accept the money — that when they came to see me and offered me cash, I should refuse it. I did that. I sat on a mat and they put a plate in front of me, but I took no money. So my father had to send them away.

Rosemary's grandmother stood by her. Because her father had beaten her often when she was a child and because her stepmother treated her so badly, her grandmother supported her on this question of an unwanted marriage.

My grandmother wanted me to do what I wanted. She had seen how I had suffered as a child under that woman...and when I refused to take the money, my aunt said, 'leave her — perhaps she is possessed by the spirit of her mother.' So they left me alone.

My uncle helped me also. One day a girl friend said, 'why do you worry so much? We'll go to a Spanish dance school and train.' So I went with her for six months; I didn't say anything to my family, they thought I was working. Then I bought a ticket to Mozambique. My father found it and took it away with my passport. He discovered I wanted to leave. So I went to my grandparents and said, 'You see, your son hides my things. What can I do? I want to go away.' So my uncle helped me get a new passport. Then I left to go to Mozambique.

Rosemary became a dancer in a night club and there she met her husband. His family, like her own father, disliked the idea of her marrying him. Eventually they went to Zambia, where Rosemary discovered her husband was being unfaithful to her. She told Judith Schulz that she had visited a n'anga, who gave her some medicine, which she placed under her husband's pillow to make him tell her the truth. When he woke up in the morning he told her about the other woman and promised to give her up. 'A Black woman, not a White woman. So I was safe.'

Rosemary's suffering was largely the product of external divisions, of being caught between different worlds and cultures.

The 'Coloured' Women

Shelagh

> It's funny. Many Whites father Black children whom they see walking about — the children have their White father's features, yet the Whites don't seem to care or notice. White wives don't see it either, not even on the farms. But where else do the Coloureds come from? (A question articulated by one Zimbabwean woman.)

Where, indeed? Shelagh, a so-called 'Coloured', knows exactly where she comes from: a Black mother and a White father. Tall, elegant, well-educated, she was trained as a receptionist and a model. She knows only too well, she says, that she would not have enjoyed the benefits of education if her Black mother had not encouraged her to adopt the status of a 'Coloured'.

The 'Coloured' community in Zimbabwe is not very large and is subdivided into several groups. There are people who are descended from 'Coloureds', others who are the result of a marriage between a Black and a White, a Black and an Asian, or an Asian and a White. There is also a small Chinese community. In the fabric of colonial society, the status of the 'Coloureds' was somewhere between the Africans at the bottom of the scale and the Whites at the top.

There were specially allocated residential areas and schools for 'Coloureds'. Shelagh's problem was that in order to go to such a school, she had to live in a 'Coloured' area. As she had a Black mother, she spent her first years in a Tribal Trust Land. Her mother decided that Shelagh should be given the opportunity to enjoy 'Coloured' privileges.

Shelagh explained it very simply.

> I was born in a Black area. When I was five or six, my mother gave me to a Coloured family, to what I call my Coloured parents. They

already had eight children of their own. I became part of that family. My mother still lives in the Communal area and now I see her about once a year. When I was adopted by a Coloured father and mother, my Black mother gave up all her rights. It was a sort of law, that once you were taken by a Coloured family, your Black mother should not have anything to do with you. But my Coloured family had bought a farm near the Selukwe Tribal Trust Lands where I was born. It was only a few miles walk away. I was born in Selukwe in 1954. I went to a boarding school and after that, I trained as a model and receptionist. I was the first Coloured person to be employed at my first workplace. I think that all they wanted was a showpiece for a receptionist. If I was given any modelling job to do, they would never show my whole body, only bits of it. You know, an arm or a leg, or something. They would never allow a Coloured to model properly.

In my second job, I was also the first Coloured person who was ever employed there. It was six months before they got a Black person to be my assistant. I realised at this place, again, what problems one has as a Coloured. The first day, tea was brought round and my tea was served with everybody else. But I suddenly noticed that they were all watching which cup I was using, so that in the afternoon when the tray came round again, none of them would use the same cup. The same thing happened when I was sitting on a bench in the company bus with these people. They squashed themselves onto two seats because nobody wanted to sit next to me. Well, the next day, I bought my own teacup.

I got married 11 years ago. My Coloured parents were disappointed that I had married a Black man. They wanted me to marry a Coloured. Today, they have accepted my husband and, of course, they have also accepted the children.

When I was small, I realised that there was a difference between the various degrees of colour. There is also a difference within the Coloured community and being married to a Black man made me more aware of what was going on. Some of the Coloureds of my generation would say things about the Blacks. It was drummed into my head that I was Coloured and, therefore, that I was better off than the Black man. It was only when I was older that I began to realise that I was Black and wanted to identify myself with being Black. You know, I am coloured because I have a Black mother and a White father. But there are Coloureds who find being related to a Black embarrassing and they think that when there are

Coloured families on both sides, they are superior to people like me. I have never met my father. I don't know who he is. My mother was a domestic worker and when she became pregnant, she came home. It could have been a plus sign for her that she had had a White lover. In some cases, you know, the women would do that just to get money and sometimes the White man would look after the child, because the child might not have been accepted by the Black family. But that was not the case with my mother. My mother gave me up because she thought it was better for me.

Fay Chung

Fay Chung, a member of the Asian community, is in charge of the Curriculum Development Unit in the Ministry of Education. Born in 1942 in Harare, she is a third generation Zimbabwean who identifies completely with her country.

We are a very small community of Zimbabweans of Chinese stock. About 400 and that includes children. We were allowed to go only to Coloured and Asian schools until recently. My father was a businessman and had a little shop in Harare. We were eight girls and one boy and we were all fairly well educated because my grandmother, an illiterate peasant from China, was really very bright. She wanted all of us, particularly the girls, to be educated. My grandparents came from China in 1904. They were of peasant stock and they came in search of land. There was a great deal of land pressure in China, particularly in the area from where my grandparents came. Most of the overseas Chinese originate from a Canton province. Only the eldest son was given what little land there was and so they had no option but to leave China. They had only heard of Johannesburg, and made their way to Africa through Mozambique. They came to Zimbabwe on foot. Originally, there was a group of 14 men and after that, the colonial régime decided to stop allowing Chinese people to enter. They were rather afraid of the 'yellow peril' invading Zimbabwe. So these 14 brought their families out and, as a result, we have this very isolated community.

I was fortunate enough to belong to a generation where there was actually a secondary school for Asians and Coloureds. It was opened in Bulawayo in 1953. If you meet Asians and Coloureds slightly older than myself, they might not have gone further than primary school. I think that this is one of the things that caused a great deal of bitterness among us. Unless your parents were wealthy enough to send you overseas, or to South Africa, you couldn't enjoy any secondary education. I remember an aunt who completed her primary school when she was 11 and she had to stay in the same class for the next five years, though her grandparents made every effort to try and get her into a school. They tried all the White schools, private and government, but they said, 'we don't allow any Chinese in this school.' So my aunt was a very frustrated woman, who had to repeat the same work constantly from the time she was 11 until she was 16. I was fortunate. I also spent two years at a convent school, where I did my sixth form, and then I studied at the University of Zimbabwe, when it was still the University College of Rhodesia and Nyasaland.

Miss Chung spoke without hesitation about becoming politicised.

Like all children, I understood at a fairly young age that certain things control our lives. I think that going to school with Coloureds politicised me. They were very much a rejected people and, from the point of view of both the Africans and the Whites, I think they were in a particularly unhappy situation. When I went to St. John's school, which was run by Dominican Sisters, it was originally intended to be a school to take care of children of mixed parentage. They were not really orphans. They were simply deserted, by both their fathers and their mothers. I saw so many tragedies. I remember that on one occasion, the mother of a young child of eight or nine came to see her and it was a Black woman who arrived. This little girl was so ashamed of her mother because she was Black. This is something that left a lasting impression on most of the children there.

In our own community, the Chinese, we realised that the big problem was land. We found ourselves unable to buy land in either the White or the Black areas. There was a constant feeling of bitterness because there was so much land around and yet my grandparents weren't able to buy any of it, even if they had the money. I remember one incident. One of our neighbours, also Chinese, had been gambling with a European. The stakes were so high that this White friend staked his house, which he lost in the game. This meant that the house had to be transferred to the Chinese and there was a terrible uproar because a Chinese actually owned a house in a White area. Being our neighbour, we saw all this happening, the reporters coming and so on. And it really seemed ridiculous that there should be such an upset simply because a man managed to get a house.

I was also able to get an insight into the position of the Blacks. After university — my first degree, that is — I went into African education. For four years I taught at Harari[1] Secondary school and that was when I understood the effect of African education and what it was all about. I was appalled to see the low level of education, the type of curricula, the quality of teachers, particularly at primary level, and also the conditions of life for the children whom I was teaching. It was quite horrific for someone like myself who came from a very protected background.

I learned a lot, of course. The sixties was a period of great violence. There were many violent demonstrations. I remember one day coming down Third Avenue and seeing the school in the throes of a riot. The churches and schools were often the targets for attack. I suppose that because we were working there, we thought we were doing a great job. What we didn't know was that the school was a symbol of oppression for the local people. It was terrifying to have the school surrounded. The police and their dogs arrived to disperse the people who were besieging us. But then, don't forget, out of five children in Harari, only one could get into secondary school — there were four bitter children, and this accounted for the anger.

The violence of those years was such that although I worked there, I could never go into Harari township in the evenings. This was particularly true of Saturday nights. The violence was, well, misdirected. There was a great deal of beating-up of women in the streets, street fighting, a great deal of drunkenness and so on. Don't forget, the colonial régime built beer halls in almost every corner of Harari and, inevitably, the confusion ended in bloodshed.

The White Women

Women in Rhodesia have played a significant part in the development of the country from the very beginning when the intrepid wives of pioneers suffered immeasurable hardships in order to make homes for their menfolk and their children in a wild and often hostile land.

This introduction to *Profiles of Rhodesia's Women*, a book published in 1975 by the National Federation of Business and Professional Women of Rhodesia, indicates the blindness of the Rhodesian Whites, especially of the women. The introduction added that:

*The heritage and inspiration of the early African teachers still spurs
many women of today to devote countless hours in the service of
others and to strive equally with their male counterparts to make our
beloved Rhodesia the finest country in the world for all its
inhabitants.*

It is difficult to believe that this was written only seven years before
Zimbabwe's independence.

But the message of *Profiles of Rhodesia's Women* should not be
ignored. Like the fiction of the White Rhodesian, Doris Lessing,
this book evokes the role of White women in colonial society — it
was colonial. The woman was not considered to be an equal to
men. The White Rhodesian woman had to be pretty, a social asset
to her man. If a White woman enters a room in Zimbabwe, White
men still rise and wait until she is seated. They will allow her to
precede them into a lift, see her into a car, will open doors for her.
The observance of such sexist niceties reflects the dependent role of
White Rhodesian women. Their only power, indeed, lay in their
control of household servants. Some women did enter the labour
force but, for the most part, their jobs — as secretaries, for
example — merely extended their role as the providers of services
to men. Those who joined a profession were seen as odd.

It is ironic that the first chapter of *Profiles of Rhodesia's Women*
should be entitled, 'Front Line Women'. It explains that:

*Phoenix-like, the new Rhodesian Women's Service has risen to back
up their men, waging war against the terrorists on our border. No
need for conscription here. The women were more than ready when
the call eventually came.*

The many photographs of pistol-toting mamas on the farm suggest
the role of women in the days of the 1970s bush war. The women
bolstering up the morale of the men who were fighting against the
'terrs', the White girl singing for the trouppies, the White pin-up:
all this was part of the effort to keep up morale, part of the
propaganda against Blacks. Women of all ages served in the police
reserves and in the various voluntary services as nurses, 'manning'
radios on farms, helping with road blocks, finger-printing,
searching African women, and similar activities. But the image of
women as pretty things was maintained. 'Some women,' according
to *Profiles of Rhodesian Women,*

Councillor Dorothy Maurira, one of the few women councillors in Zimbabwe, speaking at a session of the Chitungwiza Town Council.

*...stand up to it better than others; here and there you can see the
tell-tale signs of strain on faces, a far-away look in the eyes, a wrinkle
marking a forehead that should still be smooth, a certain tiredness.*

The White women in pre-war, pre-Independence days, had a life ·
of leisure that would have been unusual at that time in Europe.
There was no need for her to dirty her hands in the running of her
household. She did not even have to look after her own children —
servants became a kind of substitute mother. As a result, the White
woman had even more leisure time than her husband. Only a few
used it well: gardening was considered important, but garden boys
were always available to do the hard work. Women could devote
themselves to all kinds of sports, including bowling and golf. Since
many houses had a swimming pool, swimming was not so much a
sport as a basic part of life. The image of the middle-aged woman,
primly dressed in a white starched uniform and old-fashioned hat,
watching the bowls roll on her well-groomed lawns, was part of
Rhodesian society. After Independence, the bowling ladies were
blessed by the new society's policy of 'reconciliation', which was
introduced by Robert Mugabe after his election in 1980. In 1982, a
team of bowlers brought back international sporting honours and
their contribution was duly honoured. Earlier, the Whites had
cheered in 'their' girls, an all-White hockey team, who had brought
back the gold medal from the Moscow Olympics.

Only a handful of women lived with any sort of awareness of the
society around them. A few, notably Doris Lessing, used the
injustices of Rhodesian society to inform the context of their
creative work. Several women were engaged in White politics in
various parties. Others served in the civil service and in the
provision of health care but never achieved a high position. It was
only with the birth of the new Zimbabwe that women became
Cabinet Ministers, Public Service Commissioners and Permanent
Secretaries. In the totally male-dominated Rhodesian society,
White women baked cakes for their children's school fetes in the
traditional English manner, served on charitable trusts and carried
out good deeds. A few were professional women, mostly teachers,
but were not admired for any independence of thought or spirit.

The White society was a mixture of British descendants (many of
them arrivals after World War II), South Africans and a handful of
Greeks, Italians, Portuguese and Germans. They all acquired not
only the same Rhodesian accent, but also the attitudes and values
of the society in which they lived and moved.

Catherine

Catherine Lloyd was born in the same year as Fay Chung, but has had a completely different upbringing. She grew up on a farm near Hartley (today Chegutu), and was sent to a Johannesburg boarding school at the age of nine. She travelled by train to school, at first with her mother and then on her own, and was given an upbringing that mimicked the customs of the English upper class.

Although she was a bright pupil, Catherine at no time contemplated going to university or, indeed, pursuing a career. Marriage was her only aim, for which she was groomed according to the ideals of her class. She learned to play the piano, although she had little musical ability. She could ride well because of her farming background and won several prizes in the agricultural show in Salisbury. No one, she says, seemed to notice that she was very good at mathematics, but she accepts this as normal.

Catherine's husband was born in Aldershot, England. They married when she was 18 and she divided her life between what she called 'town' and 'country': that is, spending the week in Salisbury and the weekends on the family farm or at Kariba (both she and her husband are excellent yachtsmen). They own a cottage on Lake McIlwaine, a few kilometres outside Harare. They spend their holidays in South Africa. Catherine's ideals are integrity, good manners and restraint. She admires, she says, those women who come from pioneer stock. Her main concern seems to be with 'them': her servants, the 'girls' and 'boys'. At dinner tables and at the golf club, this is an ever-recurring subject of conversation, even today. The standards of White women are those of bygone decades in Europe. In the past, they organised handicraft classes for Black women, flag days to raise money for charity, Church bazaars and, in general, behaved like women in Britain's counties. Their relationship with Black women was that of 'madams and girls'. Few of them understood the traditional roles of Black women.

Elizabeth Moyo, a middle-aged widow and nurse, spoke of a White woman who helped with handicapped children in the townships in this way:

> She was a White woman like any other, friendly but detached, as though I simply wasn't there. I could not imagine myself ever talking to her on equal terms. I knew what her life was like, but she never placed herself in my position or that of my mother or my grandmother. She could never imagine the close bond in our family. To me, she always seemed a helpless sort of person, like all the other White women. They seemed to be able to do nothing for themselves, except perhaps to make a cup of tea. They didn't even

At a park in the centre of Harare.

change their children's nappies and yet they would come to our women's clubs and teach us floral arrangement or something — what a waste of time! They knew nothing about the domestic life of their servants, nothing about our problems, nothing about how we lived, what we believed in, what we thought. They didn't care. For them, we did not exist.

As Catherine herself said:

Chris was a gardener and John worked in the house, as a houseboy. His wife used to come in and do the washing for me once a week. I didn't like to have children on the premises and the children lived with the family in the Tribal Trust Lands. [Which TTL?] I'm sorry, I don't know. It's very difficult, you know, to remember these names. They were pretty good servants as far as they went, you know, but they are all lazy when it comes down to it. You have to make sure that they don't get away with too much. Everything has to be locked away, of course — you can't trust them.

I think our servants were pretty well off. I mean, we gave them rations every week and paid them well. John had Thursday afternoon off, as well as Sunday afternoon. They used to take it in turns to be on duty on Saturdays and Sundays. You know, you couldn't be without anyone over the weekend because you always had people coming, especially when the children were small.

No, there was no electricity in the *kayas*², nor a bathroom. There was a shower and I gave them a big tub and on Sundays, I suppose, they used to have their bath or something. I made sure they had plenty of soap. You know, there's always that smell about them, isn't there?

White women were second class citizens in relation to their men, but very much first class in relation to the Blacks. The White woman at the top of the social ladder would be the woman who was married to a wealthy man and/or a member of one of the pioneer families. The single woman's career might be admired, she might even be accorded some status, but she was most unusual and her work was not taken very seriously.
Catherine saw nothing wrong with the system.

Oh we did have the vote. After we were given some sort of constitution — in the twenties, I think — they brought in a franchise for some Blacks. You couldn't have votes for a Black man and no votes for White women, that would have been mad. So we got the vote.

But I don't know anyone who believes in Women's Lib. We are different, aren't we, we bear children, we have this monthly thing — you know, it takes it out of you, you can't do the same work all the time, like a man. Anyway, a woman can get all she wants from her man, if she sets about it in the right way, so what is this all about? I don't understand it, none of us do — my friends, I mean.

Life as she knew it, she said, has disappeared.

But I think we will stay. My husband has his business here. As long as it's safe, we'll stay.

She had tangible reasons for staying: a five-acre garden, a six-bedroomed house, a swimming pool, a tennis court and servants. She would be unlikely to establish such a high level of comfort in any other part of the world.

The Other Whites

Some White women, as well as men, identified with the Black cause. Grace Todd was one such woman, the wife of Garfield Todd, the missionary turned politician, who is today a Senator under the Mugabe government. Judith Acton, their daughter, is another exception. She is one of the younger generation who rejected White values, having grown up on equal terms with Black children on the mission run by her father. Today, Mrs Acton is in charge of the Zimbabwe Project, a non-governmental organisation that unequivocally sided with the Black majority during the war. After Independence, it initiated numerous projects for former combatants, which it continues to support.

Doris Lessing, born in 1919 and raised on a Southern Rhodesian farm, is a famous novelist who set out to evoke the attitudes and the atmosphere of the White Rhodesian community in much of her fiction. In her first novel, *The Grass is Singing*, which is set on a Rhodesian farm in the thirties and forties, Ms Lessing captured the ambivalent relationship between a White woman and her Black servants:

...She had never come into contact with natives before, as an employer on her own account. Her mother's servants she had been forbidden to talk to; in the club she had been kind to the waiters; but the 'native problem' meant for her other women's complaints of their servants at tea parties. She was afraid of them, of course. Every woman in South Africa is brought up to be. In her childhood she had been forbidden to walk out alone, and when she had asked why, she had been told in the furtive, lowered, but matter-of-fact voice she associated with her mother, that they were nasty and might do horrible things to her.

And now she had to face it, this business of struggling with natives — she took it for granted it would be a struggle — and felt reluctant, though determined not to be imposed upon. But she was disposed to like Samson, who was a kind-faced respectful old native, who asked her, as she entered the bedroom, 'Missus like to see the kitchen?'

She had hoped Dick would show her round, but seeing that the native was eager to, she agreed. He padded out of the room in front of her on his bare feet and took her to the back. There he opened the pantry for her — a dim, high-windowed place full of provisions of all kinds, with great metal bins for sugar, flour and meal, standing on the floor.

'Boss has keys' he explained; and she was amused at his matter-of-fact acceptance of a precaution that could only be against his stealing.

...Then came a native to the back door, asking for work. He wanted seventeen shillings a month. She beat him down by two, feeling pleased with herself because of her victory over him. He was a native straight from his kraal, a youth, probably not out of his teens, thin with the long, long walk through the bush from his home in Nyasaland, hundreds of miles away. He was unable to understand her, and was nervous. He carried himself stiffly, his shoulders rigid, in a hunched attentive attitude, never taking his eyes off her, afraid to miss her slightest look. She was irritated by this subservience and her voice was hard. She showed him all over the house, corner by corner, cupboard by cupboard, explaining to him how things should be done in her by now fluent kitchen kaffir. He followed her like a scared dog. He had never seen forks and knives and plates before, though he had heard legends of these extraordinary objects from friends returning from service in the white men's houses. He did not know what to do with them; and she expected him to know the difference between a pudding plate and a dinner plate. She stood over him while he laid the table; and all the afternoon she kept him at it, explaining, exhorting and spurring him on. That night, at supper, he laid the table badly and she flew at him, in a frenzy of annoyance, while Dick sat and watched her uneasily. When the native had gone out, he said,'You have to take things easy, you know, with a new boy.'

'But I told him! If I have told him once, I have told him fifty times!'

'But this is probably the first time he has ever been in a white man's house!'

'I don't care. I told him what to do. Why doesn't he do it?'

...The next day at lunch, the servant dropped a plate through nervousness and she dismissed him at once. Again she had to do her own work, and this time she felt aggrieved, hating it, and blaming it on the offending native whom she had sacked without payment. She cleaned and polished tables and chairs and plates, as if she were scrubbing skin off a black face.[3]

Footnotes:

1. A black suburb in the capital, renamed Mbare when Salisbury became 'Harare'.
2. Domestic living quarters.
3. Doris Lessing, *The Grass is Singing* (London: Heinemann), 1973, pp 70-71, 80-82.

Rhodesians Never Die

We'll preserve this nation
For our children's children
Once you're Rhodesian no other land will do,
We will stand tall in the sunshine
With truth on our side,
And if we have to go it alone,
We'll go it alone with pride.

We're all Rhodesians
And we'll fight through thick and thin
We'll keep our land a free land
Stop the enemy coming in
We'll keep them north of the Zambezi
Till that river's running dry
And this mighty land will prosper
For Rhodesians never die.[1]

---

1 Quoted in Julie Frederikse, *None But Ourselves: Masses vs Media in the Making of Zimbabwe,* (Harare: Zimbabwe Publishing House) 1982, p 51.

Chimurenga Song

Hark!
It Thunders!

Smith! Our brothers and sisters
Are living in the forests
Because they are protecting our land
Smith! Our brothers and sisters
Are living in the forests
Because they are fighting for our country.

They would have wanted
To sleep under a roof
They would have wanted
To till their lands
But for the love of our land
But for the love of our land

They are fighting for our land
They are fighting for our land

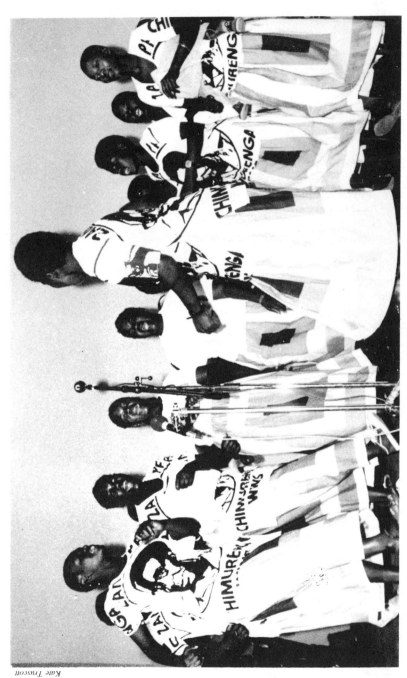

Here a group of women in Harare celebrate International Women's Day.

4

THE SECOND CHIMURENGA

In the fifties, Nationalism and Pan-Africanism burgeoned throughout the African continent. Southern Rhodesia was no exception. The many Africans who had fought for the British during World War II came back ready to struggle for full participation in the political life of their country. The African National Congress (ANC) was reorganised, and a City Youth League was founded. Africans were disappointed, however, by the creation of the Central African Federation in 1952, which was composed of Southern Rhodesia (Zimbabwe), Northern Rhodesia (Zambia) and Nyasaland (Malawi). The control of the Federation lay in Salisbury — in the hands, therefore, of the Whites. No African in any of the three countries wanted the Federation, which was equated with the oppressive rule of colonialism.

In Southern Rhodesia, two trends merged: first, the growth of nationalism among the urban people; and second, a growing resentment on the part of the rural population. Their dissatisfaction was fuelled by the diminishing productivity of the impoverished soil on the TTLs, as well as by the passing of the 1951 Land Husbandry Act which, by forcing Africans to cull their cattle, was seen as an assault on the traditional way of life. Both the urban and the rural people, therefore, were united in their opposition to the government. In 1957, the Youth League and the African National Congress merged, and Joshua Nkomo was elected as President of the ANC. Two years later, the ANC was banned. In the following year, however, a new party, the National Democratic Party (NDP), was formed, which became the spearhead of the political struggle. The NDP was then banned and replaced by ZAPU. A period of unrest, as well as of disputes within the party leadership, followed. In 1961, talks began with the British Government concerning a constitution that would lead to Independence. Joshua Nkomo attended the London talks, but the proposals were rejected by his colleagues. A year later, ZAPU was banned.

During this time, White politics were moving to the right. During the fifties and the era of the Central African Federation, the Whites had talked of a 'partnership' between themselves and the Blacks which, according to a leading White politician, was a partnership similar to that 'between the rider and the horse'. Some attempts were made to integrate the races, but they failed. The creation of a multiracial University College provoked an exodus of White youngsters who preferred to study in South Africa. Similarly, the opening of a public swimming pool in Salisbury for the benefit of all races led to White protest and to bitter feuds between conservative and liberal Whites.

In 1962, it was clear that the Federation was doomed. A year later, a surprising election result brought a new party, the Rhodesian Front (RF), to power, which dashed the hopes of the liberal Whites for any sort of peaceful co-existence with the Blacks. More repression against Black protest followed as Africans, determined to gain their civil rights, continued their struggle. Nkomo formed the People's Caretaker Party, a successor party to ZAPU, but this time, he did not take all the leaders with him. A new party was created, the Zimbabwe African National Union (ZANU), under the leadership of the Rev. Ndabaningi Sithole. For a while, the energies of Black politics turned inwards, as the two parties attempted to sort out their differences. But the yoke of oppression was by no means forgotten and, as the following testimonies show, women as well as men continued their struggle for political change.

Isn't there a saying that treason never succeeds, because if it does, no one calls it treason?

It was like that with our war. They called our armed struggle 'terrorism'. Once we had won, then it became a war, officially. Of course for us it had always been a war. First it was a war with words, political. Then it became a war with guns.

From an interview with a Zimbabwean commander

Smith's UDI in 1965 had many consequences, both inside and outside the borders of Rhodesia. Britain, the colonising power, was theoretically responsible for the welfare of Africans. However, the British and its Labour Party government badly let down Africa, much to the shock of Kenneth Kaunda, the Zambian President, who had believed that UDI would meet with severe penalties. The Zambian offer of the use of its country as a base in the fight against the 'rebels-against-the-British-crown' met with no response. The kith-and-kin argument proved too compelling for the British Government of the day, which merely embarked on a long and weary road of negotiations with the White settler government — sometimes secretly, sometimes amidst a fanfare of publicity.

The United Nations imposed sanctions, but they proved ineffectual and hurt Zambia more than Rhodesia. Neither sanctions nor 'talks-about-talks', which involved top level meetings on British warships, nor travels by the American diplomat, Henry Kissinger, brought Ian Smith to heel.

The Rhodesian Government isolated Zimbabwe's leaders in prison and detention, imposed censorship, and declared a State of Emergency. And even though the Whites were now cut off from the world, enjoying the support only of South Africa and of Portugal (until the coup in Lisbon in 1974), the UDI period was simply a continuation of colonialism for the majority of Black Zimbabweans.

For the banned political parties, it was a period of change which erupted in war. ZANU, which had already decided in 1963 that armed struggle was the only way to achieve political rights, organized an armed unit (ZANLA). A year later a White man was killed in the first military action since the Chimurenga of 1896-7. ZAPU also changed its strategy, organizing its own armed wing (ZIPRA). During the sixties, the liberation movements were still learning the art of bush warfare as, indeed, were the Smith forces. Two major battles were fought during that decade: one at Sinoia (now Chinhoyi) in 1966, another a year later at Wankie (Hwange). At Sinoia, a handful of ZANLA fighters battled it out with the Rhodesian forces, while at Wankie, both ZIPRA and cadres of the African National Congress of South Africa were involved.

Smith and his men, armed with the assistance of South Africa, defied both sanctions and the freedom movements. Rhodesian forces dug themselves into the Zambezi Valley, the only point of entry for guerrillas. But in 1971, ZANLA forged an alliance with FRELIMO and was able to open a new front in the north-east of the country. In December 1972, a White farm in the Centenary district was attacked. In retaliation, Smith closed the border with Zambia, only to re-open it once his intelligence service had discovered that the attacks came from inside Mozambique. President Kaunda, however, refused to open his side of the border, which remained closed until 1979.

The British effort at a settlement included the 1972 Pearce Commission, which was despatched to assess the reaction of the Black majority to a proposed constitution which had been approved by Smith. Pearce met with a solid response of 'no', however. Both the war and the diplomatic manoeuvres continued. Following the Lisbon coup, South Africa and Zambia embarked on 'détente', which resulted in the release from prison of the Zimbabwean leaders and the signing of a 'unity accord' in Lusaka between the various nationalist parties. This did not lead to peace, however. Instead, the bush war was intensified. In 1976, an abortive conference was convened in Geneva by the British, in another attempt to solve the problem.

It was South African pressure which made Smith accept the inevitability of Black rule. He reluctantly handed over the reins of government — though on his own terms — to a 'moderate' Black government led by Bishop Abel Muzorewa. Only in 1979, following protracted negotiations between Smith, Muzorewa and ZAPU/ZANU (which had formed an alliance in 1976 known as the Patriotic Front), was an agreement reached in London's Lancaster House. This led to elections in March 1980 and a victory for ZANU (PF), led by Robert

Mugabe. Independence followed in April 1980.

The war was hard for both Blacks and Whites. Smith extended the claims of military service, so that by 1979, every White male, irrespective of age, was subject to call-up. Every man was either a member of the police or of the army reserves or served in the army itself. White women, too, became involved in various auxiliary services; farms became walled fortresses, and every Black was now considered a potential 'terr' (as the freedom fighters were called). After 1972, Rhodesia was a country at war. Many Whites left — 'gapped' it, to use the local expression — usually going 'down south'. A curfew was imposed and so-called 'protected villages', known as 'keeps', were established in order to isolate the guerrillas from their natural bases, the villages. Any 'curfew breaker' was shot. Cars could only travel when they were escorted by army vehicles.

The valley war had been a silent war, largely unnoticed by the world at large. But the bushwar became an international issue, highlighted by the missionaries' descriptions of the atrocities committed by the Rhodesian forces. White Rhodesians, brainwashed by years of propaganda, remained loyal to 'good old Smithy'. The war displaced millions of Black Zimbabweans. Many fled to the edge of the urban areas, where they lived the difficult life of squatters. Others crossed the borders into Botswana, Zambia and Mozambique. Schools closed: after 1976, more and more young people fled, not to escape the fighting but to join it, as members of either one of the freedom movements.

The Rhodesian forces combed the countryside and bullied the villagers, all of whom they suspected of 'running with the terrs'. As the majority of Zimbabwean women lived on the land, and as the majority of the rural population was, in any case, composed of women, it was the women who sheltered and fed the *vakomana*. Women carried ammunition under their everyday loads and used their children as messengers for the fighters. Their suffering was terrible. Their huts were raided, their men were taken away, they were beaten, raped and massacred. The 'keeps' became concentration camps, from which they had to walk many kilometres daily in order to till their fields. Those who returned late were shot as 'curfew breakers'. Rhodesian forces followed the refugees across the borders, bombed and raided camps, and killed thousands of people. The Selous Scouts, who were trained specifically to fight in the bush, were notorious for their cruelty in the rural areas. Missionaries who helped guerrillas were arrested and many of those who were allegedly murdered by 'terrorists', may well have been killed by Selous Scouts.

In 1979, a cease-fire was arranged at Lancaster House. The British opened 15 assembly points, which were 'manned' by British policemen, army officers and Commonwealth observers, to house the freedom fighters during the run-up period to the elections. These final months of the conflict were a period of stress for everyone: for the freedom fighters, the political parties, the Rhodesians and the British. But they brought an end to a long and bloody war that had cost countless lives.

Women and the War

Elizabeth Moyo reminisced about the role of women in this bitter struggle.

As I said, my mother comes from Manyika Province. She lived in a village not far from the border. She says she remembers the ZANLA attack on the farm in Centenary, which started it all.

One night, she was called out. We don't knock on doors, we clap. Someone clapped outside my mother's door, calling her to a meeting. She said that there was a good deal of dancing and singing, and that it was a women's meeting. The n'anga was there and a woman who was a spirit medium. No, n'angas are not spirit mediums, they are traditional healers, though of course they can sometimes be possessed. That woman was not a n'anga. She had come to pass on a message. It came from the spirit medium of Nehanda and it was very important. It told the women they should open their huts to the boys.

At the beginning, nothing happened. The boys who had come in, the *vakomana*, had crossed the border. They never slept in the village, they just came for food, and no one ever asked them any questions. They were fed, they were there, and then they were gone. It was strange to see young men around the village playing with the dogs, going out in the morning when the boys were driving the cattle out. It had been a long time since young men were in that village. One morning, they heard an unusual noise. Later they found out what they were — helicopters. They came in, I don't know where they landed, but they came in. They went through that village like cockroaches...no, like locusts. Locusts eat everything that is in their way. And that's what the soldiers did. They went through the village, they pulled women out of their huts, they made them lie on the floor with hands outstretched. The children, some of whom were tied to their mother's back, were crying, but it made no difference to the soldiers. They pulled my grandmother out of her hut. They threw her pots all over the place, breaking them. Then they took four of the young women and took them away. The

Kate Truscott

Here women in the Wedza Communal Land are collecting water for the Ruzane Women's Garden Project.

villagers could hear their screams. It went on for hours. And then, the next morning, one of the Black soldiers who were with the security forces came in and said, 'You can go and get them.' They got into their helicopters and went away. The women were dead. They had been tortured. When the Smith forces talk about political consciousness, it's a joke really. How else can you get politically conscious? Unless it's through incidents like this. Some weeks later, the soldiers came back. This time, when the helicopters came, many people ran away and hid in the bush, but the soldiers found them and drove them back to the village. They made them get on to lorries, told them to pack a few pots and other things. When the villagers asked where they were going, they were not told. But this was one of the first keeps that they were taken to. You know the keeps, the villages that they put up to break contact between the *vakomana* and the local people. My grandmother spent three years in a keep.

According to the Whites, the peasants had 'asked to be placed under protection from the terrorists' and willingly moved into the 'keeps'. Nothing could be further from the truth. Keeps were concentration camps, enclosed by barbed wire and under constant surveillance. People were herded together, utterly disrupting the pattern of village life. The keeps were set up for security reasons, without any thought for the welfare of those who were allegedly being protected.

Indeed, peasants were removed without warning from their fields, crops and cattle. As a strict curfew was imposed, the long walk to fetch water and wood, and also to look after the gardens, proved too much for many women. As a result, food was in short supply and, as it was forbidden to plant food in the spaces around the thatched huts in the protected villages, they not only looked like concentration camps, but served the very purpose of such camps to those who were forced to live in them. Every inhabitant was carefully registered, every entrance and departure checked. The water buckets which the women brought back from their endless trips to wells and watering places, for example, were inspected. Babies were even removed from their mothers' backs in order to ensure that no parcels were being carried illegally. Keeps were used only after 1972, when the 'hot war' started: at first only near the border, and then generally throughout the country, as guerrilla networks spread. The objectives of the Smith forces were first, to isolate the *vakomana* and stop the peasants from feeding them, and second, to stop further recruitment for the war among the peasant community.

Elizabeth recalled that:

One day I had to visit a sick relative near Shamva. The keep was called Gono. About 16 villages had been cleared, so around two thousand people were in that keep. An aunt told me that they were very worried, because their dip tanks had been destroyed and the cattle had strayed, heaven knows where. Each time she came back from her garden she was searched. She was old and sick. It is hard for a woman like that to walk 20 kilometres a day. If she was late, she could be shot. They shot at everything at night. A lot of what they called 'curfew breakers' on the radio were killed in those days. Not freedom fighters, mind you, just people late from their gardens.

Such things were common in the latter years of the war. The following is an account of an attack on a village, after a *pungwe*, an all-night session with freedom fighters.

The village was asleep. The cattle lowed softly in their corner of the kraal. In one hut, a little girl called Tandi stirred. She had malaria and had been restless all day. Her mother and her aunt had fussed around her in a way they only did when children were sick. She'd enjoyed this. Usually it was just, 'Tandi, it's time you went down to the river. Tandi, have you been to the water hole? Tandi, go and fetch your little brother. What do you mean, not looking after your brother, eh?' But tonight, her head ached and she could not sleep.

Tandi was 11 years old. She had been to school for two whole years and could read and write. That was considered enough. Her mother needed her after that and so she came home. She knew this was the custom and she settled down without complaint. But sometimes, like tonight, when her head ached, things did not seem so easy. She glanced around her. The others were asleep. She thought she heard a bird call — or was it a hyena? The cattle lowed again in the kraal. She knew that somewhere, water had been left for her to drink, perhaps she should get it. It might make her feel better, her throat was so dry, her head felt so heavy, her limbs sore. She rolled out from under the blanket, carefully made her way to the door, and opened it. It was a bright moonlit night. She blinked and saw the moon over the thorn bushes, towards the hills at the end. Clouds drifted across the sky and covered the moon. At that moment, someone grabbed her, placed a hand over her mouth, and pulled her down to the ground. She was terrified and she couldn't utter a sound. Her limbs seemed to have turned to water. Then a voice whispered in her ear some words she understood. They were home words, Shona words, not like the English words taught at school. So she knew these were her own people. What did he want from her, this man? 'Little one, little one, go wake your mother,' he said. 'Go tell her we're here, tell her quick.' The hand was removed from her mouth. She replied, with a little laugh, 'I'm sick.' 'We are all sick, child. We will be sick until Zimbabwe is free. Go. Go get your mother.'

Tandi scuttled across the bare space in front of the hut. Her mother was awake, and at the door. 'Child, child, what is it?' 'They're here,' said Tandi, 'they're here. The *vakomana*, they are here.' Silently, the woman disappeared inside the hut and within minutes the village was astir. Someone picked up Tandi. She felt a liquid pressed to her lips and drank it, as her throat, parched and sore from the fever, gratefully swallowed. All around her was silent activity. She could hear it in the dark and she knew. It was not the first time the *vakomana* had come, the soldiers who had come to free her people and Zimbabwe. She knew of the dangers, too. She had heard the women speaking. Now her mother and the others were busy cooking, preparing food. The *vakomana* would be hungry. They would have spent many days walking in the bush.

The young man who had picked Tandi up came to look at her. 'You are sick, child. Perhaps one day, when you are big, you can come with us.' 'I will come now,' she said shyly, 'I am big. I am 11 years old. I look after my brothers. I am big.' 'I know you are. One day we will make you a soldier. And one day, perhaps after that, you will be a wife.' He laughed and went back to his comrades. Suddenly, someone began to sing. Within seconds, everyone seemed to have gathered at the baobab tree in the centre of the village.

The man who had first seen Tandi, Khami the commander, picked her up once more and placed her in his arms. He began to sing and the others sang with him.

> *Zimbabwe, Zimbabwe, we love you.*
> *Zimbabwe, the country,*
> *Zimbabwe, the land.*

Tandi was too ill to understand, but she was happy squatting in her blanket at the feet of the comrades. Over and over again, the villagers repeated the words. The singing never stopped. Someone brought beer, which was passed around, and finally Tandi fell asleep. 'At night, Zimbabwe is ours,' the *vakomana* said. 'In the day, the Whites still rule. But the day will come when Zimbabwe is ours, day and night.'

Near the hill known as Makumbe, was the Hill farmhouse. Here too, people were awake. Three police reservists arrived at about the same time that Tandi was woken in her village. Usually, no one travelled at night, but these men had come because they were trailing a group of 'terrorists'. They had been told that there were some in the area and were instructed to take the group of 'terrorists' by surprise, rather than using the usual means of communication. Ten Selous Scouts had arrived previously and had stayed at the Hills' home for two days. Now that the police reservists brought them the news of the presence of 'terrs' in the area, they were jubilant. 'Those gooks,' said one of them, a young man of 18, 'Those gooks, we'll fix them.'

Just before dawn, the people at Makumbe sat down to the sumptuous breakfast prepared by Mrs Hill: eggs, bacon, fresh scones. She still kept to the customs of the old country and added a few of the new. There was fruit salad with pawpaw, the lush produce of her back yard. She gazed at the young men fondly. 'It is time,' they said. And she thought, 'time to live or time to die,' but she knew there was no answer to this and in her heart she was afraid.

The Selous Scouts, including three Africans, were tough, trained and seasoned in bush warfare. They knew the signs and could read them. Slowly they made their way towards the village where Tandi was lying in restless sleep. The guerrillas, the *vakomana*, had posted a sentry outside and he, too, could hear the signs. Silently he raced back to the village and ran into the centre of the dancing and chanting crowd — as soon as he was seen, the command to scatter was given. The people ran. Some went into the bush but already it was too late. The Selous Scouts knew their work well. There had been many encounters. This was the fourth year of the bush war and they knew exactly what to do. Hand grenades, flares and tear gas canisters were thrown into the village. The people screamed in panic. Again, Tandi was snatched up, this time by her mother. The child, handicapped by her illness, tried to run back into the hut, delaying the flight by a few precious seconds. A bullet, perhaps only a splinter, caught her mother's throat and opened it, like a laughing mouth. It was too dark for Tandi to see what had happened, but she knew it was something terrible. All around her were smoke, screams, and the crack of gunfire. Tandi never did find out how long the battle went on, but she knew that she had to run and keep running. The bush was alive. Animals, as well as people, were running away, terrified by what was happening in the village.

The Selous Scouts had encircled the entire village and those who had not managed to get away, were doomed. Khami rallied his men and they fought back bravely as they retreated into the bush. This was one of the most difficult battles he had ever fought. He knew why the Whites were so angry. The week before, his own section had fired two rockets into a little town nearby and he had heard that in Salisbury, in a department store, two bombs had killed 11 people. War. Sometimes you won, sometimes you were killed, but in the end there would be only one solution: Zimbabwe's Independence.

No time, now, to try and trace the informer who had told the security forces about their presence in the area, but when this was all over, they would find him. Oh, yes, they would find him and they would kill him. His death would not be pleasant. All through the war there had been traitors, people who ran with the Whites, people who still thought the Whites were strong, that they had a magic which could not be matched by the freedom movements.

But Khami had no time for such considerations, only time to load and reload his AK47. They were good, these Whites. He shouted, giving commands to his people, telling the villagers to move quickly and let the cattle out. No one heard. The young man sprinted to the enclosure and out ran the terrified oxen and cows, the wealth and pride of the kraal, stampeding in terror. Snorting, they headed for the bush, allies in confusion. An ox was hit and his entrails opened, as in a sacrifice. Khami had no eyes, no ears, except for the enemy. He picked up a burning branch and threw it on top of the hut in which the girl Tandi had tried to sleep earlier that night, causing the flames to shoot up and sweep over other roofs. Good. It would warn other villages in the region; comrades, too, would see this glow and they would know it was not the dawn.

Down at the river, even the crocodiles seemed to have vanished. Khami worked his way towards the fall-back position, which had been identified before the visit to the peasants. How many had been in the village, 60 perhaps? Not all would be caught. There were nearly always some survivors. He moved cautiously. Suddenly, he saw what looked like a blanket, and realised almost immediately that it was a child. She was squatting at the foot of an anthill, wide-eyed, silent, unable to move. As he drew close, he knew who it was. The same little girl. She stared at him with unseeing eyes, then looked back at the red glow. He nodded. Taking her hand, he pulled her to her feet and pointed silently in the direction ahead. Equally silent, she rose and followed him with the obedience that she had been taught. Tandi, the little girl from the village, who had lost her community and her mother, was on her way to become first a refugee and, in time, a soldier.

This story was told by Elizabeth Moyo, who heard it from her daughter. Elizabeth believes that one should forget the horrors of the war. She said, 'Africans are not bitter people. We like to forget. We do not dwell on the horrors of the past. I hate no-one. I don't think we should hate. Hate is destructive for ourselves.'

Ruvimbo

Ruvimbo talked about the role of women in the struggle. In an interview during the war, she said:

> Women were more politically conscious, more revolutionary and more involved in the armed struggle, because the war was happening in the rural areas — where the women were. The men only heard about the guerrillas being at home if they returned for weekends or for the holidays. And even if there were men in the

villages, the young guerrillas tended to trust the mothers in the village, not only because they were women, but also because they had been less exposed to the settler régime. Of course, a woman always feels motherly towards any young boy. Anyway, that is the way it started. It gave the woman a head start, as it were. In 1973, many people went to the north-east, where the guerrillas were, to help carry material. They were attacked by the security forces and were unable to protect themselves. They were carrying all the material, the messages, and if the helicopters or the army forces came, or jets bombed them, there was no way in which they could return the fire. So they demanded some training in self-protection. Once the women were in the bush, they couldn't return because they had been exposed. So it happened that in 1973, the first women were trained in exactly the same way as men. That meant that when they were out in the bush together, the men could no longer say, 'You cannot do this [whatever it was] because you are a woman.' They were shedding blood together. This is the bond. This is what revolutionised the role of the woman in Zimbabwe.

In another interview, Ruvimbo said:

The participation of women in the armed struggle has shown that women suffer and are oppressed not only because they are women. During the war the women of Zimbabwe realised that their oppression was to do with the system, the colonial system.

The women who were trained by ZANLA had quite a different role to that of the women who were part of ZANU in the political days. The trained woman guerrilla is a guerrilla in the same way as the man. Imagine when a woman arrives as a fighter in a village. When the people see a woman who has been fighting the enemy, it impresses them tremendously. It became one of the most important methods of mobilising. A man would say, 'it's impossible that a woman should fight. I must do the same.'

There are, of course, prejudices that are difficult to overcome. Imagine a group of 2,000 men who suddenly have a camp commander, aged 23, who is female. Traditionally, they have been taught that women are inferior, and now their female comrades have to tell them what to do. What happened was that they were as good as, if not better than, the men. So you might have experienced the following: A woman gets up at four o'clock in the morning to train. The men, who on average are 35 years old and strong, say they are tired after a while. The woman says nothing, but she continues to train. You can be sure that this impressed the men tremendously. Our five best commanders were females. If there were 20 male and five female commanders, one could be sure that the five females would have to be better than the men, because they had to prove themselves. They had to prove that they could do it. And this is the case with all prejudices. They have to be overcome, and they can only be overcome by hard work.

Camps in Mozambique and Zambia were frequently attacked. On 9 August, 1976, for example, Rhodesian ground forces were led to a refugee camp in Nyadzonya and, as the photographs of the mass grave show, a terrible massacre took place. Another attack was launched against a major camp at Chimoio in November, 1977, at a time when diplomatic moves to settle the Rhodesian question were yet again under way. It was a massacre: 100 people died, 600 were wounded and 20 were unaccounted for. One of the survivors was Ruvimbo. She talked to me soon afterwards in Maputo, in an interview that was published by the *Sunday Times* of Zambia on 13, August 1978.

It was, she said, a nightmare, 'a harrowing experience that is difficult to erase from my mind.'

We were all in one place in this transit camp with almost 8 to 10 thousand people, waiting to be distributed to various refugee camps. We were not military people and I am not a trained person. I was simply working as a teacher.

On the morning of the attack, she said, the refugees had assembled in the open to discuss the various chores of the day in the camp's maize fields, schools and clinic. She added:

At about seven am, we saw a plane very far off in the sky and we started arguing about whether it was a civilian transport plane or a military reconnaissance plane.

For safety's sake, it was decided that all the people who had gathered to plan the day's work — about 2,000 of them — should disperse quickly to their various chores so as not to attract the attention of the plane.

But before they had time to do so — before the children had even entered their classrooms — there was a loud explosion. Somebody shouted that the camp was under attack and told the people to hide.

It was such a surprise, and because we are not military people, we just didn't know how to protect ourselves. We didn't know whether to gather all the children together, or let them run the best they could...

There was complete confusion and everybody ran wherever they could. I did not run far, I went into a small bush and decided to keep down for a while. As the jets bombed, all we could hear were trees splitting and bombs dropping. We looked into the sky. It was just grey and green, full of explosions, fire and smoke. I could not believe it.

For 20 minutes, the camp was strafed with bombs and bullets. The mothers, children and elderly men who worked on the farm, ran in all directions with the other refugees. Most of them were mown down by helicopter bullets.

When there was a lull, I ran towards Chimoio, which was safer, as the other side was in the direction of the border. I raised my head a bit and looked towards Chimoio, but there above the trees, I saw green parachutes coming down.

She could not make up her mind where to go. She could not run into any of the huts as the Rhodesian forces were notorious for burning down the shelters with their occupants inside. 'I just decided there and then,' she said, 'that I would hide in a pit latrine, and I ran. The bombing had resumed, but I ran towards a toilet nearby and I dropped into the pit. But I could not drop further than my shoulders as I got caught in the hole. After I raised my hands, I was able to go down. I fell on my back and thought that perhaps I was wounded.'

The faeces came up to her waist. But what was most repulsive, she said, was the maggots that immediately started crawling all over her body. She feared that she would be eaten alive by them, a death that would be slower and even more painful than that caused by rebel bullets. She leaned against the wall of the pit and resigned herself to hearing the bombing and the whining of the bullets above her head. At the same time, the helicopters that hovered over the camp dropped paratroopers, who cut down every moving object with their automatic weapons.

The bombing, gunning and burning of the homes went on and I could hear the crackle of fire all day and night till the third day. I did not feel hunger or thirst. I was just waiting and I think it was just that kind of passiveness that saved me.

She said that on the third day, she heard the footsteps of people running about the camp. She tried to listen to the voices but could not hear anything because of the flies. Then, tired and thirsty, she tried to drink her own urine, but could not do so because it was very bitter. She was saved, however, by the heavy rain that came. At first she tried to trap the water with her tennis shoe, but it was impossible.

> Then I saw a plastic bottle floating on the waste, and I took this, cut off the top to make it bigger, and used it to catch some water. I was able to catch four inches of water but it was very dirty. I drank it as I was afraid the rains might stop and I wouldn't have anything.

On the fourth day, .she dozed off and dreamed. Then she was awakened by the sound of an engine she could not recognise.

> I listened and heard the noise drawing nearer until it came right to the camp and I heard its vibrations. I called out, but my voice must have been very small as there was no response. I called again when the engine noise was a bit low, and I heard footsteps and a voice in Shona.

She then saw FRELIMO and ZANU guerrillas peeping down the hole with guns. She called out to them not to shoot her, telling them her name. They pulled her out and took her to a nearby mission hospital, which was already crowded with the injured survivors of the raid.

Mavis

> My name was Mavis when I was born, but I changed it to a Chimurenga name, Banga. This means 'knife'. I wanted to be like a knife, to cut down the enemy. I joined the struggle when I was 15. We had heard a lot about *gandangas* (bad people). The White soldiers used to come to our village and talked to the Headman, who told us to be careful of *gandangas*, the terrorists who, he said, killed people for nothing. We knew very little about the war. All the people in our village were women, apart from the Headman, who was an old man, and two of my uncles, who were also old. My father worked in Salisbury.
>
> One night, my mother woke us up and told us we had to go to a *pungwe*. I didn't know what that was and I was afraid. My sister, who was younger than me, cried. At the *pungwe*, we found many people from other villages. In the middle were *gandangas*, only now we didn't call them that, these were comrades. They were dancing and singing slogans and soon we, too, were singing and shouting. They told us about the war, about why they were fighting and how we were oppressed. About a week later, they came again.

After they left, the Boers came and punished us. They took away the Headman and I never saw him again. My aunt was beaten and left as dead. All these terrible things made me want to join the struggle. The next night, I took some food and I and two other girls left.

On the way to the border we met some Rhodesian soldiers, but they took no notice of us. Later we found out how lucky we were. At night, we slept in the bush and early in the morning, we crossed the border. On the other side we met FRELIMO. They were cross, because there were no comrades with us, just us girls. But later they were nice and took us to a camp, where we found others. That was how I joined the struggle.

Bertha

Bertha was a young girl of 12 when her village was destroyed by bombs.

It was terrible. People were crying and I saw an arm, all by itself. My mother was screaming for me and I had my brother with me, but somehow we did not die. Many people did. We hid in the bush and that night, some comrades found us and told us we had to go with them.

Our village was near the Botswana border. Of course, I did not know this. I did not know what a border was, or another country, I did not understand even the bombs. We had been happy, my mother and my father and then my brother and me. I always had one good meal a day, because I had helped to cook since I was five years old. My mother said, 'if you work, you eat.' I worked and so I ate. I was in standard four when the village was bombed. I never found out what happened to the school. My father was in town when we were attacked.

When it was night, we walked. In the day, we hid in the bush. Sometimes we were thirsty and hungry. I think we walked for three nights. So much has happened, I don't remember everything. Some things, of course, I'll never forget. I was frightened when we met animals at night. Once we saw a wild pig and the comrades said they would have shot it, but a shot might have been heard, so they left it. I was sad, because I would have liked some meat. We only had berries and some water carried in bottles by the comrades.

We even met some cows on the way. The comrades said that the cattle were straying because of the war and that the people in Botswana were not happy about this, which was why there was a fence. When we saw the fence, we would know that we were in Botswana. We didn't see a fence — perhaps it had been cut down — but we did get to Botswana. Some police came and took us. My feet were sore and bleeding and my little brother was very sick. My mother carried him some of the way.

People asked us lots of questions, sometimes the same ones, all the time. But we did go to a camp and had food and drink. After some weeks we went to Zambia in a big plane. I stayed in a camp with my mother until I was taken for training and joined the struggle.

Siyathemba

On 17 October, 1978, a women's training camp in Mkushi, 150 kilometres north of Lusaka, was attacked by Rhodesian forces. ZAPU stated at the time that there were 1,589 young women and 36 children in the camp. The bombing began at 11.00 in the morning and was followed by the dropping of parachutists from helicopters. The ground forces cut down the women mercilessly. At the same time, Rhodesian forces attacked another camp near Chikumbi, about 20 kilometres north of Lusaka, where about 100 women and girls were killed and 90 badly wounded; some 200 were reported missing.

Siyathemba Mlilo was one of the survivors of Mkushi. Her story, told in a ZAPU booklet, is hair-raising. She had fled to Zambia with her brother, because their father had been arrested and they, too, feared arrest. She was 19 years old and undergoing medical training, when the enemy struck.

I saw about five jet fighters and six helicopters, some of which dropped Black and White troops at the edge of the camp. Some of us ran away and hid in a cave near the river bank. We heard a whistle and a little later, we saw our teacher, Jane, who called out to ask why we didn't come out of hiding, whether we hadn't heard the whistle. She said there were some people in the camp who wanted to talk to us. Some of the girls decided to come out. I stayed where I was, because I was suspicious and afraid.

After the others had gone, I looked out. I saw a group of about 80 to 90 girls in front of eight to ten White soldiers. One of them gave Jane a gun and told her to shoot the girls. Jane refused and I saw how they first murdered Jane and then the girls. I think that about 50 were killed. The others managed to escape to nearby caves and ditches. The racists then threw grenades into the hiding places and the girls were literally torn apart. Meanwhile, I managed to run away and hid in the bush. Two White soldiers ran past, but didn't see me. Then a Black soldier saw me and to my surprise, he only took my hat and said in Ndebele, after he had made sure that no one was watching, *Bakelu uyele. Akulabantu, Uyasingi* [Run along there. There is no one there and you'll be safe]. I was badly burnt by napalm, but I managed to get to a village and the people took me to a nearby police station.

Muriel

Muriel said that one night, her whole school was taken away by the comrades. She was 14 years old and knew all about the war. Comrades had come often and so they were doing little work at school. It was a mission with a hospital, and the missionaries were giving treatment at night to the wounded comrades. For this reason, they were rounded up one night and told to leave. It was no longer safe for them to remain, because the Smith forces would find out sooner or later about the missionaries and would beat and kill everyone.

About 200 children and teachers left. Some were lost on the way or drifted towards a village. Muriel was one of a group of 30 who made it into Mozambique. There, everything was quite different from what she had expected — she had thought they were marching to freedom and riches, not to a refugee camp with no blankets and little food. However, huge trucks with beans arrived the day after she and her party had reached the camp and once, they received clothes as well. She learnt to sleep rough and said that she is grateful, not only because it made her realise how lucky she had been at school, but also because it made her self-reliant. Once she had volunteered to teach the younger children, she made friends and was taken seriously by the commanders. After six months, she was moved from the refugee camp to a military camp. She fell in love, she said, with a comrade who became her first lover. But sadly, they were posted to different assignments and she never met him again. Later, she heard he had been killed in a contact.

Muriel added that she was proud to have been able to take part in the struggle for Zimbabwe.

Oshiler

'A fierce battle,' said Oshiler Chikuhuhu, 'was fought between the 20 and 23 September, 1978, in a Mozambique transit camp'. She explained:

> This was a man to man fight against the Smith régime, which resulted in the death of many enemy soldiers and ZANU and FRELIMO comrades. The battle lasted for three days. The operation took place both on the ground and in the air.

> We woke in the morning as usual. The weather was misty and cold for only a few hours. That was from 3.00 to about 9.30 in the morning, when the weather suddenly changed and became fine and sunny. We were sitting at our posts as usual, when suddenly two spotter planes came. This was not a surprise because we knew that we could be attacked at any time, and we were always prepared. We were scattered over a large area and the enemy was in the middle. No fire was heard, until the spotter planes started bombing randomly into obvious terrains, so that they could hear where our fire was coming from. Fire was heard from every post. Within a few minutes some jet bombers, followed by Canberras and helicopters, started bombing. Some petrol bombs lit fires which burnt fiercely. What else could we do, except return the fire! Within a few minutes some of the planes were burning.

> A Dakota, the plane which deployed ground forces, was shot down and all the soldiers who tried to escape with parachutes were killed. The helicopters had returned, followed by the Canberras and then the jet bombers. The two spotter planes remained behind. Once again firing ceased, until the planes started to bomb. Those operating heavy artillery then returned the fire, with the result that our strongholds were spotted. By this time, it was about 11.30 in the morning, and the bombing went on until about 2.00 in the afternoon.

> The jets returned, using different tactics. The enemy had discovered that our radius was very big and began to bomb fiercely. The sky became dark with the smoke of bombs. The situation grew worse. But we never lost hope, although our comrades were dying. The jets bombed from about 2.00 when the helicopters tried to drop ground forces. But they didn't get a chance. There were 28 helicopters and two Canberras. I found it hard to count the number of jets as they travel at such terrific speed. Some of the helicopters were shot down. After failing to drop the ground forces, the planes disappeared at around 6.00.

On the second day, the planes came at around 6.00 in the morning and started bombing. As before, we returned the fire, but the situation was very tense. The planes wouldn't leave, bombing from the moment they arrived until 6.00 in the afternoon. They managed, too, to drop their ground forces. Many comrades died, because it was difficult to fight both in the air and on the ground. We never gave up, though! We kept on returning fire until the planes left.

The ground forces remained and this was dangerous because it meant that we might shoot at comrades by mistake. The planes returned at the same time on the third day and began to bomb. FRELIMO comrades realised that we were getting tired and gave us reinforcements. They brought a Cuban tank, which destroyed some of the planes, and the others left at around 2.00 in the afternoon. The ground forces remained, simply because the helicopters did not manage to pick them up. We followed and destroyed them. During the battle, the enemy had dropped some time bombs which were set to explode at different times. Some exploded as late as a month later. We moved to a new camp, as we were afraid of the time bombs.

This was one of the worst and most intense battles fought in Mozambique.

Tainie

It is hard to imagine the Tainie Mundondo of today with a gun in her hand. She sits behind a desk in a Harare publishing house, smiling and confident. The phone rings, she answers, waves towards a chair. Yes, she is prepared to talk about herself. What was it we wanted to know? It was a very long story, she said — there was so much to say.

At the time I joined the struggle, I was very young. I was born in 1958 in Mutare, where I went to a boarding school. When I ran away, I was only 16 years old. I think I was simply adventurous, and I'd heard so much about the war. Our leader, Chitepo, had just been murdered and one of our teachers gave a very exciting speech about him. As a result, 12 boys left that night. They were supposed to be going to a meeting in Mutare, but actually they took a bus to the border. The police arrived and searched our rooms, asking us all sorts of questions. Then we talked about only one thing: how we could get to Mozambique ourselves. I hardly worked at that time — in school, I mean.

One student knew how to get there, but he thought that this was only something for boys, not girls. Then it was Easter. The bus fare was too expensive, so I stayed at school for the two weeks. I went to see the teacher who had given that speech and asked him to help me get across the border. He refused, but I kept on at him and eventually he told me to go to that boy I have already mentioned. He advised me to wait until I had finished my exams, so that I would get a good job later on. But I was determined to go. I gave some photographs of myself to a friend, for my mother. My friend cried.

I managed to get out of school without anyone seeing me. Unfortunately, when I got to Mutare, I met a man who was in love with me and had bothered me for some time. I told him I was visiting my brother. Finally I found the boy, who was already on his way to the border with some others, and I persuaded him to take me along. We sent back some younger children who ran after us. We took a bus and walked for two hours, arriving at the border at about eight pm. We saw some FRELIMO soldiers. The boys told me to speak to them and say I was with my brother. When they saw my four brothers, they arrested all of us, but I wasn't worried.

We laughed and were happy to be in Mozambique. They took us to a camp. The next day we left for Rutende, arriving three weary days later. After that we went to Chimoio, where we stayed until Mozambique's Independence in 1975. After that we had some tough weeks in Tete. There was never enough to eat and there were some comrades who refused to accept girls as freedom fighters.

I worked as a primary school teacher in a camp in the north of Tete. I had been chosen by some comrades for this job. Later I received military training. It was difficult, because I had to carry on teaching and had very little time. So I was a bit behind during the training, but I eventually learnt to be a soldier. We were 200 trainees with six trainers. After that, from August 1977 onwards, I spent time in various camps. Once I concentrated on domestic affairs as I wanted to write an instruction manual, but I was transferred to the education department in Beira. Several of the camps in which I stayed and which housed refugees, were bombed. In December, I was sent to Denmark for further training. It was hard work. We had to design our own textbooks, study agriculture, learn typing, and other things. In 1979, I went back to Maputo, and was then sent to Tete and made responsible for distributing books and information material. When I came home in 1980, I wanted to be a teacher.

Instead I found work at the Reserve Bank, but I found it boring. Now that I work as a responsible editor, I am happy.

There is something I want to say about life in the camps: there was no difference between men and women. If there was any job to be done, like fetching water or wood, both men and women were detailed to do it, although fetching wood and water is traditionally women's work. There was only one difference: men were better trained in the use of arms than women. They were also issued with more weapons. But a woman officer was treated with the same respect as a man.

If one was in love, this could cause a problem. I was unlucky, because the man from Mutare who had been in love with me, suddenly appeared in one of the camps and said I belonged to him. He said that after I had disappeared, the security forces had come to see him and had asked about me. That was why he, too, had had to leave. I had to explain to the comrades that I had nothing to do with that man. My parents did not know him and the last time I had met him, I had only been a schoolgirl.

Naturally men and women fell in love. If they wanted to stay together, they reported this and they were registered. Family planning was not possible. It would have been wrong to have birth control when so many people were dying. Many children died — the struggle was hard for them. Pregnant women had a tough time. They were taken to a special camp for women and children. We did not talk about *lobola*. If we were in love, we felt free.

I am very happy. I have my husband and one child. We who were in the struggle know that things are not yet going quite the way we wanted, but we know that it takes time for everything to change.

Sister Janice McLoughlin

An important figure in the liberation struggle was a Catholic nun, Sister Janice McLoughlin. After Independence, she returned to Zimbabwe and worked for the Zimbabwean Foundation for Education with Production (ZIMFEP), on a project to resettle hundreds of refugee children in a special 'farm school'.

Sister Janice did not set out to become part of the Zimbabwean struggle. It happened because the Smith forces began to develop special tactics in the bush war. A commando group, known as the Selous

Scouts, had been trained in guerrilla warfare and the art of disguise. These soldiers, Black and White, committed many atrocities in the villages and mission stations. The Catholic Commission for Justice and Peace set up an office in Salisbury to monitor such atrocities: murder, rape, the use of chemical warfare, the burning of crops, and so forth. The energetic Sister Janice joined this Commission. Born in 1942, in Pittsburgh, Pennsylvania, Sister Janice grew up in a caring family. Her mother was a teacher and her father a carpenter who worked as a casual employee in the coal mines. 'He used to come home at night,' said Sister Janice, 'and talk about the terrible conditions in which people worked and lived. He was active in the workers movement; though trade unions were forbidden by his firm.'

> I developed very early on a feeling for inequality between rich and poor. When I was still small, my brother used to take me along to lectures, and I remember a Jesuit priest who talked about civil rights. That was long before Martin Luther King. At that time I also read Albert Luthuli's book *Let My People Go*, which impressed me very much.

In 1961, Janice McLoughlin entered the Order of the Maryknoll Sisters. She decided to go to Africa and, once permission had been granted, learnt Kiswahili and worked for seven years in Nairobi. In 1977, she went to Rhodesia. Later she was arrested and deported because of her work for the Justice and Peace Commission. She maintained contact with affairs in Rhodesia, however, and worked hard to publicise the liberation struggle in the United States. Returning to Africa, she went to the refugee camps in Mozambique, the only White ever actually to live inside the camps. She said:

> When I began to work in the Commission in 1977, I immediately made contact with people in the rural areas. I think we knew much more of what was going on than the authorities. The rural people trusted us and told us about the atrocities of the security forces, about the conditions in the keeps. The official propaganda never mentioned the liberation movements. The press only reported atrocities perpetrated by the 'terrorists'. So for three months I collected reports by informants, who took great risks by coming to us.

> I remember one young boy who told me his story. He had been dragged to the police. They gave him nothing to eat or drink, and beat him until he became unconscious. After a week, they released him without any charge. After he had told me all that, he showed

me his back, which was one entire bleeding wound. Although he had spoken to me quietly, had told me everything in great detail, he must have been in great pain. The boy must have known that he could have been killed for reporting the story to us. But he also knew that publication of the incident would help the struggle.

The members of the Commission were also at risk. We were always being threatened. Our African fellow workers were eventually arrested. I began to realise fully what the struggle meant. After I had been there for three months, the police turned up. They had been in the office before but this time, they had a warrant. They first searched the office, then our home, to look for what they said were publications that would 'arouse fear and despondency'. I had not expected them to search my home, so they found my diary with comprehensive notes. I knew what would happen. They would arrest me as a suspected Communist and supporter of 'terrorists'. That same night, they took me to Chikurubi prison near Salisbury, where I stayed for three weeks.

Almost all the Black prisoners were political detainees — several hundred. There were three or four so-called 'Coloureds', who had been imprisoned for some minor offences, and also three Whites who had stolen some money. I was supposed to be in solitary confinement, but I managed to have some contact with the other prisoners. Prisoners know how to get around regulations. I was well treated from the first day onwards. The Black wardens said to me, 'You know, we support the *vakomana*, but we have families, we need a job.' Female prisoners smuggled letters into my cell, and when they found out that I was to be deported, they gave me notes so that I should know how they were being treated.

In prison there was the same racial discrimination as outside. Blacks received the worst treatment, conditions for 'Coloureds' were slightly better, and Whites were better off than anyone else.

After three weeks, I was taken to court on charges of supporting 'terrorists'. They asked me if I supported terrorism and I replied, 'I support the liberation struggle and I don't call that terrorism.' I was deported to the USA. I had intended to return to Kenya, but some Zimbabweans came to me and said, 'You mustn't give up the struggle now. Help us by telling the Americans what is really happening at home. They don't believe us, but they will believe you.'

So I stayed where I was, gave many lectures, wrote a lot, worked with members of Congress and the Senate, and received a great deal of information from the Commission in Salisbury. They were always under pressure but were never actually banned. They were threatened but they were never charged with anything. In 1978, I went to Mozambique, together with some Afro-American journalists. I met the ZANU leaders. I will never forget when I met Comrade Josiah Tongogara, who died just before Independence.

We were at the airport and someone asked if I wanted to meet Tongogara who happened to be there as well. Naturally I wanted to, but I was a bit nervous. What would he say? That I should keep out of their affairs, that it had nothing to do with me? Someone introduced me and Tongogara embraced me. Then he took my arm and stroked my skin, saying, 'You helped us prove that the colour of the skin makes no difference. We have told our fighters that we are fighting not the Whites but a system. Now we can say, look, there is a White who supports our struggle, who even went to prison for us!' Then he asked me to send medicine and equipment for the refugees, saying they needed even food badly. So I returned to America for a year and after that I worked in the camps in Mozambique.

Food was always a problem in the camps. It was originally thought that the war would not last a long time and, of course, the refugees were living in other people's countries. They did not feel free to use the land, though in some camps they did establish some fields and gardens to grow their own food. Naturally, they built their own shelter, but they needed materials for this, as well as fuel and clothing. The liberation movements were openly supplied with arms and equipment by socialist countries. The aid supplied by non-governmental groups in the West included mobile clinics, medical equipment, blankets and clothing. But on the whole, the people had to manage on their own, which was not an easy thing to do.

Sister Janice McLoughlin worked in the educational section in Mozambique from 1979.

In August 1979, I went to Mozambique and worked very closely with ZANU's Department of Education and Culture. ZANU had set up a refugee support committee of which I was a member. We met regularly, we'd assess the needs, buy supplies with the money which we'd received from the Zimbabwe Project, and then take this to the camp. I spent some time at Matenge camp, at ZANU's educational headquarters. I was so impressed with what they were doing during such a difficult period. There was very little food, little clothing, poor living conditions, but, in the midst of all this, they had developed a new and revolutionary educational system, the same that we are now trying to implement here in Zimbabwe. They were really doing education with production. They actually had teacher training courses in progress. They had administration courses, primary and secondary schools, cultural activities, plays — everything was going on in the middle of the war. I was very privileged to be able to be there. They still tease me about it. They say, 'You were the only White ever allowed in our camp, the only one who ever stayed with us.'

Mrs Zvobgo (who, together with Mrs Mugabe and Mrs Nhongo, was responsible for Women's Affairs) worked for five years in the headquarters at Maputo in Mozambique and in the camps themselves. It was her job to travel to the camps and find out what the women, both combatants and refugees, needed — such as cotton wool, sanitary towels and baby nappies. She explained:

In the camps we set up courses for the women, particularly in the one where we kept our expectant mothers and nursing mothers with the children and babies. When women combatants became pregnant, they were moved to these camps. Of course, in theory there should have been no sexual relations at all between combatants, but you can't really make rules about this. If you do, you find that the rules are broken. Well, once a girl was pregnant, she had to move from the guerrilla camp and do you know, the women really hated moving to the special camp. I never realised how much they hated it until they were told to go and then they treated it as a punishment. I used to try and explain to them that it was for their own good and for the child, too, because in this camp they would be given proper food, special food. But they never really got used to it....We didn't go in for family planning. We didn't restrict people's emotions. We felt that family planning was something that had to be decided by the parents, and that such things should only be introduced once we had got back home. Of course I talked to the girls privately and told them to look after themselves and how best to do it. But there was no overall policy on family planning as such.

Given the tremendous strain that everyone was under, it is not surprising that traditional beliefs assumed great importance. It was believed, for example, that there should be no sex before an action, on the grounds that this would stop a gun from going off. In theory, male comrades were not allowed to cohabit with any village women. This was a rule which was often broken, particularly in the latter part of the war, when a cease-fire seemed imminent — that it was a matter of months, rather than years, before the shooting would stop.

Joyce, a former commander, also spoke about the special problems experienced by women.

> Firstly, it was traditional that men should be obeyed by women. Secondly, it was unusual that women should be fighting alongside men and have the same rights. But when things went right, that is to say, when discipline was good, when relationships were good, women began to feel not only equal to men but the same as men. The question of sex did not arise. They were able to move with comrades, irrespective of sex. Where difficulties arose, it was often with leaders, with leading comrades, who felt it was their right to demand the services of women as semi-servants or semi-wives at their base camp. A number of women would go along with this, either because they loved the man, or because they felt that they could gain some advantage from an association with a leading comrade. This led to problems with other comrades. The exploitation of female comrades was one of the grievances which cropped up in disputes betwen rank and file and commanders. The first time was during the quiet period in Zambia, after the first battles in the Zambezi Valley. Little was happening then except the regrouping of forces and the re-assessing of strategies, and so on. Later on, we again had such problems. It was no one's fault. That's how men and women are.

The army commanders had another problem. They had to decide on the extent to which they should interfere with tradition. About one million people were in refugee or other camps outside Zimbabwe. This was a very large number of people, particularly in relation to the population as a whole, which was no more than seven million. Since many of the people in exile were young, lacking the familial guidance and support to which they were accustomed, decisions had to be made about relationships between young comrades. Mrs Zvobgo explained:

> There was one rule, and that was that there should be no prevention, no contraceptives. Once two people decided that they wanted to get married, they would have to go to their commander and the commander, in turn, would refer the couple to the Registrar of Marriages. The young people's request would be noted and they would be informed that their people at home would be told in due course, in case there should be *lobola* payment and

other traditional rites to be performed subsequently. And so the comrades lived together as man and wife.

But living together in a camp, under the conditions of war, was by no means easy. People were moved around, after all. They rarely stayed together very long.

Education in the camps, as Fay Chung explained soon after Independence, was a priority.

> Visitors who see our farm schools today, run under the Zimbabwean Foundation with Production (ZIMFEP), think it's rather awful to see the children living in such difficult conditions.[2] But do you know, these kids have an independence and clarity of mind which is difficult to find anywhere else. This is because they are refugee children who have survived really traumatic conditions in the refugee schools in the camps in Mozambique and Zambia. They think they are living in rather plush conditions now. You know, of course, about the big attack on Chimoio in November 1977. After this, we were very careful and we split up the schools. I was at a school called Paschingwe. One morning, at about a quarter past eight, our school was attacked in an air-raid. It wasn't a big school, we had only about 1,200 children. And we were fortunate. Only two children died in that air-raid.

All the camps had schools. In some cases they were primitive, while in others, there were qualified teachers such as Fay Chung or Ruvimbo. What was lacking, naturally, was a syllabus and teaching materials. Given this, it is amazing how much was achieved and how much solidarity was felt by the refugee children — which, happily, carried over into their schools after Independence.

The war ended with a cease-fire in December 1979. The political parties had never abandoned the possibility of peace through negotiation. The British, painfully aware of the 'Rhodesian problem' and their kinship with the Rhodesians, tried time and again to resolve the impasse. Margaret Thatcher attended her first Commonwealth Conference in Lusaka in 1979, following rash public remarks about the so-called 'internal settlement' between Ian Smith and Bishop Abel Muzorewa, which was considered illegal by the rest of the world. To everyone's surprise, she pledged her support for a full constitutional conference in order to settle the Rhodesian dispute. She had, it seems, been persuaded to do so by both her Foreign Secretary and by a strategy devised by Australia, Tanzania and Jamaica. The result of the Lusaka Commonwealth Conference was the Lancaster House Conference a few months later, which eventually negotiated the cease-fire agreement.

The cease-fire brought great changes for the refugees and the freedom fighters. The former were to be repatriated, in time for the elections, while the latter were to be herded into the 15 assembly points. British army personnel were despatched to bush destinations to await events — and the thousands to come — with tents, soup kitchens and footballs.

At first, the bush fighters merely trickled in. General Josiah Tongogara, who had negotiated the cease-fire with Smith's officers, had warned that it was not like the pull-back of conventional troops. Lines of communication were slow and unsure. Many were afraid that leaving the bush for these camps would be nothing other than walking into a trap. In order to inform as many as possible of his officers himself, Tongogara travelled to the north of Mozambique after his return from Lancaster House. While there, he died at the roadside when his jeep struck a stationary vehicle. His death was a tragedy for Zimbabwe.

In the assembly points, the British played cards and kicked footballs. The Rhodesians gleefully rubbed their hands: if the 'terrs' overstayed the deadline, well, they'd have it coming to them, wouldn't they? The deadline was extended. Then, suddenly, they emerged: they came out of the bush, heads held high, marching, singing, dressed in uniform, proudly shouldering their guns — some 50,000 in all. Naturally there were some 'incidents'. Equally naturally, not all the freedom fighters actually went to the camps: some were needed to help with elections, while others stayed out because distrust was still rife.

'*Mujibas*, that's what they are, messengers, those-who-ran-with-guerrillas,' claimed some Rhodesians. To some extent, this was probably so; but the hard core of the men and women in the assembly points were seasoned bush fighters. Later, when the elections had been fought and won (to the chagrin of the Rhodesians) by ZANU (PF), making Mugabe Prime Minister designate in terms of the Lancaster House Agreement, the British started their exercise of training the ZIPRA and ZANLA units as conventional forces, and integrating them into one national army. Those who remained behind still totalled thousands. They had to find a means of transition from war to peace, from fighting to civilian life. It was a slow process, with both men and women remaining for many months in the assembly points. Yet here they forged new links and formed the basis of co-operative living, which was to serve many in good stead once they had been properly demobilised. Each received a small sum — $185 a month for two years — to help them make the transition.

As for the refugees, they returned as quickly as they could. The United Nations High Commissioner for Refugees helped to co-ordinate the massive exercise of emptying the camps in Mozambique and

Zambia. Eight thousand children alone came back, who had no community to return to and whose parents were dead or missing. These children were settled into what became known as the ZIMFEP 'farm schools'. At Lancaster House, it had been negotiated that both sides in the war should be given full and equal respect. But while the Rhodesian forces were to return to their barracks, the freedom fighters (who did not have any barracks) had to go to these makeshift camps.

It was a tense situation for both the guerrillas and the Rhodesians. Both had learnt to distrust their enemy. It was hard for the freedom fighters to trust the regular troops, and hard for the Rhodesians to accept 'terrs' as soldiers. A number of incidents occurred. The Rhodesians, for example, attacked some of the guerrillas who made their way to the camps a little after the cease-fire deadline, and there were some further attacks on White farms. The whole of the election campaign, indeed, was marked by violence. But on the three days in early March when the people thronged to the polling booths, peace was kept. The freedom fighters, dressed in full uniform, marched up to the polling booths in single file, halted, gave a salute and a hoarse war cry (to the consternation of the British bobbies[3] manning the booths), voted, and silently vanished into the bush. It was hardly a 'normal' election, but one to be remembered.

Caroline was one of the combatants who entered an assembly point.

In Mozambique, in the camp where I worked, a rally was held in December 1979. That was after Comrade Mugabe and the others had been at Lancaster House and had arranged a cease-fire. At the rally we were told that we would be going into Zimbabwe, but we were not told why. We thought we were going to fight. The man who addressed the rally was a member of the Central Committee. We were about 500 or 700 comrades. So we took all our arms and, of course, we were dressed in combat uniform. We crossed the border and then we were told to enter an assembly point. It was all explained to us, but we were very frightened. Many people thought it was a trap and refused to go. In the end, only 50 of us went, following a member of the High Command. We went to an assembly point near the border called Dendera-Dalta. The people there were Australians and British, about 25 of them.

We were told not to mix with them. We stayed on one side, they on the other. Dendera had once been a hospital, but it was destroyed in the war. We slept on the ground at first. After a week, they sent a plane which dropped blankets and food. We built shelters for ourselves with poles and dagga — then just when we had finished doing that, they brought us some tents.

We were still very frightened of being bombed. So we only slept in the camp — during the day, we went into the bush. Some of us were sent to look for the comrades who had refused to come and finally, most of them joined us. Later, we spent our day doing different tasks. We cooked, fetched wood and water, acted plays and had lessons on political subjects. We never mixed with the monitoring forces.

In March, when the elections came, we went to vote. There was no polling booth in the assembly point, so we had to go out. There we found the British policemen at the polling booths. Once we had voted, we returned to camp. We were delighted when we heard the election results. Everyone was happy and we had a high party. They sent us meat and beer and we celebrated all night.

After Independence in April, we thought we could go home to our parents, but we were sent to a farm near Goromondzi. I was deployed after that in Matabeleland South. But at that time we were afraid of ZIPRA, so we did not move around much. In January 1981, I went to work at ZANU Party Headquarters in Harare in the finance department. When I left to go on a course, that was really the end of the war for me.

Footnotes:

1   See Appendix i

2   This statement was made in 1981, before dormitories were built in all the eight ZIMFEP farm schools.

3   The British had flown in members of their blue-uniformed, helmeted police to help with the elections. Most of them had never been out of Britain and for them, it was a great adventure 'in the African bush'.

Freedom

Freedom is the
Eagle in the sky.

Freedom is hope
Soaring high.

Freedom is the name
of our struggle

Freedom is sweet,
Just, eternal;
like love, life
trust, like Zimbabwe.

Mavis

After Independence, the Supplementary Feeding Programme organised mother and children groups to improve the nutritional status of the under-fives in rural areas.

5

THE THIRD STRUGGLE

...it is time for the third struggle.
Everyone should be prepared for it.
Fathers and mothers
sons and daughters of Zimbabwe.
We must struggle with all our hearts...

Struggle, struggle, you are the only way
to get genuine independence.

Caroline

Women after the War

And so they returned: men, women and children. They came back from fighting, from the refugee camps, from assembly points, and from the urban squatter camps. They also returned from overseas universities and jobs in other countries. Two million people returned to build a new Zimbabwe. After the first euphoria, this proved to be a harder task than had been expected. It could not be otherwise. A country exemplifying an uneasy mix of colonial and traditional values cannot be transformed overnight.

The specific problem of the status of women could not be instantly transformed, either, though serious attention was immediately given to the question. The government established a Ministry concerned with community development and women's affairs, placing a former female combatant at its head. It also set up a Ministry to deal with the resettlement of land. The ruling party, ZANU (PF), turned its attention to the improvement of women's skills, so as to increase their earning capacity. Other women's organisations were formed, and some of the foreign aid was channelled into areas relevant to women. Self-help and self-sufficiency became the new aim.

The problem areas were clearly identified:

Education: Women did not have the same educational background as men. The Riddell Commission found that in 1981, 32% of women had attended school for three years or less. Only 26% of men had received so little education.
Health: Women worked arduous hours, bore many children and, in the colonial period, often had no access to health services.

Many crops, like this farmer's maize crop in the Matsai Communal land, Masvinzo, were completely destroyed by the drought of 1982-83.

Training: Few women had any skills. Government extension officers had concentrated on male peasants, despite the fact that women formed the majority of rural producers.

Land: Traditionally, the land belonged to all the people, but it was the male who controlled it during his lifetime. Women worked the land, but had no say as to what should be planted or sold.

Lobola/roora: The system of the bride price is deeply enmeshed in traditional society. Women were divided in their views. Some felt that it gave their husbands the right of permanent ownership over them. Others pointed out that women for whom *lobola* had been paid, were assured of their value to their fathers and husbands. This issue proved a source of perpetual controversy. Young couples also began to resent the exorbitant rates set by parents for *lobola*, which could be as high as $2,000-$3,000 for an educated girl.

Inheritance: According to custom, it was the man's family who inherited the man's possessions, which included his wife and children. In urban society, only the possessions were desired, which caused hardships for the woman. In rural society, it was not unknown for widows and divorcees to be considered useless appendages — sometimes they were sent away, only to become destitute.

Children: Traditionally, the man had guardianship over his children. This, too, caused problems in a changing society.

Legal status: The status of White women was determined by Roman Dutch law, which was introduced by the colonial rulers. According to this law, married women could own property but were not allowed to manage it. White women were only able to overcome this problem by obtaining a pre-nuptial contract, which allowed them to act in their own right. African marriage was subject to the Native Marriage Act, under which both traditional marriages and Christian marriages could be enacted. While Whites, subject to Roman Dutch law, had benefited from the 1928 Married Persons Property Act, this did nothing for the Black woman, who remained permanently under the control of a male.

Independence sharpened the divisions: between urban and rural life, between the educated and the uneducated, between the old and the young. The young women who had fought returned to the cheers of the multitude and the silent disapproval of the family, particularly the male members. Older women, too, resented the younger generation. They had been taught that submissiveness and obedience, coupled with the bearing of many children, was the road to respect. The new young woman, having grown up in a military camp and mixed on equal terms with young men, was often ignorant of village customs and did not fit into traditional society. There was also another dimension, that of the young woman who had married abroad. In other, less male-dominated countries, her husband had been her partner, not her master, helping with housework and the children. Once he had returned home, however, he conformed to the norms of society. Wives were left more on their own, with no helping hand in the kitchen or at the children's bedtime. Many of the men felt ashamed of their earlier participation in 'women's work'.

As Africans at last stepped into the positions so long withheld from them, so their life styles changed. Understandably, the demand of 'we want it now', became frequently heard. This spilled over into the former 'townships', where young men and women, some still at school, yearned for the 'good things': cars, big houses, and meals in restaurants that were formerly for 'Whites only'. Conflict was as inevitable as change.

The Combatants

There must be change to some extent: under the old Zimbabwe system the man, as the hunter, held the gun. In the struggle, men and women participated equally, both held guns and some women were promoted to high rank. We can't push them out. There will be both men and women in all sections of our army.

Josiah Tongogara, November 1979.

There are many women in Zimbabwe's National Army. Many joined up straight from the assembly points. They enjoyed courses, learnt typing and other skills, and have become valuable members of the army and of society. In December 1984, there was a trainee woman paratrooper and a trainee engineer, both 'doing very well'.[1] But not all could find posts in the army. Some former combatants became secretaries, others joined co-operatives, supported by the demobilisa-tion allowance paid by the government. Those who married former comrades, like Catherine Katsande or Tainie Mundondo, feel relaxed in their relationships with men and also with their families. Others live on their own, often with children. A few have accepted traditional marriage and re-adopted the traditional roles of meekness — 'in order to survive', as one woman put it.

'At first,' explained Julia Zvobgo, 'the young combatants had many problems. They had left their village and parents when young. They had led a different sort of life and felt equal to men. They returned to a society where the woman was totally subservient to the man, and the housework and care of children was her business, quite apart from work in the fields (if she returned to a village) and work she did not even know how to do. The lifestyle she had learnt during the war was not accepted. Sometimes the former male comrades also rejected them. They left them. They even left their children and looked for women who had not been in the struggle. I can't say exactly, but I think that about 1,500-2,000 trained women fighters returned from the war. I'm not talking of those who had been in refugee camps, only of women combatants. We in the Party and the National Women's Organisation help where we can. We train them, we organise courses for them, we have set up the Melfort training centre, and others go to Silveira House. There was a special course for former combatants held at Ranche House. The Zimbabwe Project also helps. But, of course, it is not only the combatants who need help. The whole structure of society will be changed — *must* be changed, in order for women to enjoy the fruits of Independence.'

Ex-combatants like Caroline share her view. This is what she said on the subject of what she called 'the third struggle'.

Life in Zimbabwe after the war is hard. It is not what we expected. We had been told in Mozambique that when we returned home, there would be good land for the people in the rural areas and in the towns, we could all live in good houses.

After I had worked at the Party Headquarters, I was sent to an adult literacy course. As a former combatant, I received $185 a month. I thought it was a lot of money. I had never had any money before. In Mozambique, and also during my time in the assembly point, we had been given food and shelter. Later, of course, I understood that $185 is not much money if you're living in town. I married a comrade. He paid *roora* for me, in the traditional way. I think this is right. My brother received the *roora*, because he is responsible for me. The demobilisation money helped my husband and myself to get the house in Harare where we live now. At first, we were in a two-roomed house in Chitungwiza, which was much too small. Now we have people — comrades — living in our house, to help with the rent. We also have a nanny who looks after my two little girls while I work. Both my husband and myself work all the time, but it is still hard for us to earn enough.

When we came and looked for jobs, people asked for our certificates. But I had joined the struggle before finishing Form II, so I had no certificates and could not get a good job. After the adult literacy course, I taught adult literacy at Arcturus mine. It was very hard work and badly paid. So I looked for another job and was sent to the Government Printers, where I was trained for three months. I am now a bookbinder. But in order to earn enough money, I must work overtime in the evenings and at weekends, which leaves me with very little time. But I still want to go on with my studies. First I am going to finish my Junior Certificate, then I will try to get my 'O' levels. My husband received his training in Malta. The party sent him there before the end of the war.

I know that there is a long struggle ahead if we want to make Zimbabwe a better place for our children.

Dorothy's Return

We met the old White woman when we stopped the truck. The comrades had painted 'Nehanda' on both sides, although it was army property and they had no right. But we think Nehanda is also army property, part of the national army, a part that we prefer to the former Smith soldiers who are also integrated into this national army.

My thoughts were elsewhere, not with Nehanda, not with the old regular forces. I certainly hadn't been thinking about an old White woman. We had driven along, happily singing Chimurenga songs, all the way from Great Zimbabwe. We are based on a farm nearby. Now we were almost at the village we had come to visit, and one of the comrades said I had to walk from here.

There she stood, the old White woman. She stood next to her car, an old farm vehicle that was armour-plated. Farmers had armour-plated their vehicles during the war, to protect themselves against the landmines that we used to plant. We used to look for cow dung and then carefully place the mine under the muck or under the thick grass which grew in the centre of the farm roads. The chassis of heavily-laden vehicles often touched the grass when their wheels trundled along on either side of the dirt tracks. Then, when the wheels made contact with the dung, or the chassis with the grass, that was the end of the journey. Later, the farmers stopped driving over cow dung and protected the chassis with armour plates.

I jumped down from our truck. The White woman looked at me. Her skin was dry like the earth in a drought, and her eyes were also dried out, with no colour in them. She looked at me. She never turned her eyes towards my comrades, but looked at me, at my new fatigue jacket, at my cap. Did she know I was an officer? She looked at me and I refused to turn my eyes away. Why should I? She was an old White woman. My father and my mother, never mind my grandfather, would have turned down their eyes and mumbled 'madam'.

She looked at me and I knew that she hated me. Had her son been killed, maybe her daughter too? I wanted to shout at her and tell her that our sons and daughters had died first. My brothers and sisters had died, I saw them die.

It is time for reconciliation and we should reach out to each other. She said not a single word. I said not a single word. We looked at each other across the dirt road. My comrades shouted at me and drove away. She opened her car at last and climbed in, slowly. I took my shoes off, because it was so hot and the walk would be long — it was easier to walk barefoot. We would cross the fields away from the path which led to the White woman's farm. Refusing to turn round and look, I walked on, carrying my shoes in my hand and the things I had brought for the village on my back. The village was on a hill and the climb was hot. A small boy on a bicycle too big for him rode towards me. He screamed and dropped the bike, jumping off, because he was too tiny to reach the brakes. He left the bike where it was and ran. I laughed out loud. Now they would know. Children and dogs often announce the arrival of strangers. All was still. I could hear only the insects. During the war it had also been quiet, except for the fighting, but I never listened to the insects, like now. More children. They ran, yelling, into huts, but they didn't shut the crooked doors. I knew they were watching me through holes in the wood. A dog sleeping under a msasa tree went on sleeping. I saw it all and yet saw nothing. My heart beat loudly, perhaps the walk had done too much. No, no, I was in training, at my peak, I had run 3,000 metres easily only the day before.

Everything was as I remembered it and yet it was different. I was different. I had left as a child and returned a woman. A woman who had seen death and caused death. A woman who had looked another woman in the face and, even though she was old and White, did not quiver. Was there no one about? Only children and a mangy dog? I walked on and saw that the régime had been here. The walls of the huts were patterned with bullet holes, and three huts were gaping shells, with the roof gone. Had the husband of the old White woman been here? Her son?

An old man leant on a stick and watched me. He did not recognise me, but he was the brother of my grandfather, a son of the same father, but another mother. I dropped my shoes and took the pack from my shoulders, greeting him with a curtsy, as is the custom. Gravely he returned my greeting and someone came out of a hut to say *Mangwanani* (Good morning). After that, it was only a matter of time until I sat in my mother's hut, on a mat. She cried, although she said she was happy, so very happy. 'I knew you were not dead. I knew.' Suddenly we heard the ululating of voices — the women had come to greet me. I was the first in the village to have come home, the first freedom fighter they were able to greet. 'You are thin,' said my mother, 'You must eat well.' I remembered many days when there had been no food, other days when there was food but no time to eat, only time to hide from the helicopters. 'We must go to the n'anga,' my mother told me. 'We must cleanse you of the evil you have seen. The *vadzimu* will tell us what we must do.' The women danced and sang, while my mother looked at me and the dog outside slept on. I shivered although it was hot in the thatched hut: there were holes which my mother was too weak to mend.

I had lived in barracks, laughed and shared jokes with men, eaten with men who were my comrades and whose commander I had been and whose officer I had become. But here I was nothing. Only a girl who had come back and who had to be cleansed of blood, who had to pacify the spirits of the ancestors. The women went away. They would be back. I knew that. My mother's arm was soft. It had all been different from what I had thought. First the old White woman, now the *vadzimu*.

In every society, it is only change that is constant: everything flows, influenced by a changing environment and the challenges of other groups. Society adapts to change and finds solutions to new problems. It is impossible, therefore, to say that 'this is African society', without clearly defining which society it is and what its stage of development. In Africa, there are basic patterns which are common to the culture developed on the continent. There are differences too, not merely in language and custom, but in the development of institutions and beliefs.

Scholars are still researching the rich history of Zimbabwe through archeological and other evidence, to determine the nature of the people who lived in this region over the centuries: the hunters of the Stone Ages, the less mobile societies of the Early and Late Iron Ages. As more evidence emerges, so the country's history can be accurately recorded and the roots of its culture better understood.

The impact of outside interference, however, has been clear for a long time — first by the Arab traders on the East African coastline, who were displaced by the Portuguese, and then by the openly aggressive occupation by the BSAC in 1890. As a result, African society was forced to respond to unexpected challenges. Christian beliefs clashed with traditional religion; old customs, such as polygamy, which had answered several social problems adequately, were suddenly made undesireable by the invaders. In pre-colonial society, everyone was answerable to the family. The family, in turn, was answerable to the village, and the village to the tribal authority. In this way, no one was independent — man, woman and child were subject to the authority of the family as a whole. Individualism was not encouraged; if it did surface, it was suppressed.

The Whites who colonised Zimbabwe failed to understand this jurisdiction of the whole family over every single individual. They misunderstood the nature of collective responsibility and misinterpreted such major issues as the role of the woman, whom they saw as simply subservient to the male, and the purpose of the system of *roora* (as in Naebele) or *lobola* (as in Shona) — that is, the custom of paying tne bride-price. The belief in the ancestors was considered 'superstition', not as part of a deeply religious feeling. Missionaries, too, misunderstood polygamy. They considered it morally wrong, failing to realise that a senior wife was a very important person, often anxious to pass on sexual duties and other responsibilities to junior wives. All women played a major part in the process of production. Children, as well as age, gave the older women status, and the younger women helped their elders in the fields and in the home, just as their children helped them. The newcomers, seeing only the drudgery of women's lives, did not understand that the man, as the hunter and provider of meat, had another role, which was arduous and full of danger.

Zimbabweans resent not only the changes wrought by the imposition of foreign laws and the dispossession of their land, but also the misinterpretation of their system of values. The impact of the disintegration of traditional values under colonialism was felt acutely in the subtle change in attitudes to *lobola*. By introducing money into the transaction, the system became debased. The father began to charge cash as well as cattle, particularly for the second part of the contract, which concerned childbearing. Marriage arrangements became commercial contracts and the man, who sometimes felt aggrieved by the sums charged, used it as a reason for beating his wife. In a report published by the Zimbabwe Women's Bureau in 1981, rural women voiced some of their views on this matter.

One woman complained: 'Because my husband paid *lobola* for me, he says he owns me. He thinks he can do what he likes with me. He treats me like dirt. *Lobola* could be a good thing. It could protect us women.

But because our fathers do not want to return the cattle or the money which has been paid to them, they think that we have been sold and they will not take us back home or help when our husbands ill-treat us. We find it hard to be divorced. Our own family no longer wants us, though we have brought them money and cattle. They cannot return this, because they need the cattle for living. The old bonds are gone.'

This was the point: the old bonds had been loosened by the new ways, the new standards. As Aeneas Chingwedere wrote:

...since 1890 we have become commercialised, every aspect of lobola has become a matter of money. Figures became more exorbitant. I am not surprised to hear a young man saying that he has been ordered to pay something in the region of $,000 by his father-in-law! Today we even pay for the education which was given to the daughter...this implies the son-in-law refunds the father for what he has spent on the girl. This is against custom: we have become moneymongers...what is really happening is that we are destroying the potentially good relationship between a young man and a young woman, who are establishing a new family. Therefore, we are also destroying the relationship between in-laws. A great deal of change was brought about in the tradition: it is not tradition which is changed, but the attitude to it. We have become mercenary and this has been the influence of the Whites.

In the past, *lobola* and the extended family system worked. In the later years of colonial rule, only the shell of traditional society remained.

Women and the Law

'An African woman, whether she has been married by solemnisation of a customary marriage or a civil marriage, is a minor until she is divorced or widowed. She leaves the guardianship of her father and comes entirely under the protection of her husband.'

The Women's Guide to Law Through Life
University of Rhodesia
April, 1979

The final indignity for women was the White man's legal interpretation of African Customary laws. As *The Woman's Guide to Law Through Life* stated, Rhodesia was a country with two kinds of laws: 'the Law of Rhodesia and African Customary Law. The Law of Rhodesia is based on Roman Dutch Law, imported from the Cape at the time of the occupation, but which has been considerably modified by enacted law over the years.' Shona and Ndebele traditional law was similar, with only the Tonga, 'being a matrilineal people...differing considerably especially in woman's property and land rights.' Customary law was applied in civil, criminal law in other matters. So the law had it both ways: it described the Black woman as a permanent minor, but if she was accused of crime, she was not protected by her minority status.

African women were subject to an African Law and Tribal Courts Act regarding their minority status, property, custody of children and inheritance. People could marry under the terms of the African Marriage Act (that is, traditionally), or by a civil or Church marriage under a Marriage Act. A woman was considered a minor throughout her lifetime, so she had to have a guardian's permission to marry, irrespective of her age. A widow or divorcee was, on occasion, considered legally 'emancipated' — that is, a major. It would be difficult to find such instructions in the Civil Marriage Act to the White woman.

The woman's legal status as a minor deprived her of such basic rights as entering into a contract, renting a house in her name in a township, opening a bank account, and raising money. Everything she did had to be approved by her father, husband, brother, or other male relative. Everything she earned belonged to another person. 'Just imagine how it hurts to suffer, working on the land which doesn't belong to you and all the money I get from my crops is kept by my husband,' stated a woman in the report of the Zimbabwe Women's Bureau. Another said:

> If I was a man, I wouldn't have to ask anyone permission to do what I want to do. But my husband is in charge of everything I do or make with my hands, which is so rough and cruel. He says that the *lobola* he paid to my parents means that he bought me. So I have to follow his orders and work for him and his family.

Age of Majority

It will not be good enough to pass progressive laws and then expect everything else to follow their natural course. Laws are made for people and the people — the ordinary people out there in the villages — should be educated about their rights in order for them to exercise their rights. Only when people begin to exercise their rights can the important institution of marriage be made happier.

The Herald Editorial, 10 December 1984.

They held up their banners. They danced and clapped and ululated. When the first of the dance groups that had been arranged came onto the stage, they joined in. Later, when the speeches and the formalities had been completed, they themselves took to the stage. The excitement was infectious. It was not the summer heat that raised the blood pressures. The atmosphere was justifiably heady. For this was 10 December, 1982, the Day of Zimbabwean Women, celebrated not only in Harare's Stoddard Hall, but all over the country. December 10 would always be a special day. This was the day that, with the passing of the Legal Age of Majority Act, the disability of minority status was at long last removed for the women of Zimbabwe.

Anyone who had reached the age of 18 was now legally considered an adult, and could vote, enter a contract, own property, deal with it in any way he or she chose, and open and operate a bank account. The rope which had tied a woman to a man from birth to death, was now cut. Minister Teurai Ropa Nhongo was unable to be in Stoddard Hall, but her speech was read for her. The new law, she said, was designed to improve family links. It was based on the United Nations principles of human rights intended to ensure that no one should suffer discrimination on account of sex, race, religion or political views. It was difficult for a woman to lead a life in modern society if she was under the tutelage of her relatives. Even after the death of her father, a woman had been answerable to a male relative, an uncle, or a brother, even if he lived in some remote part of the country.

The women in Stoddard Hall held their posters high. 'We want a fair share of the Independence Cake,' said one. Another pointed to unfair taxation, which discriminated against women. True. It was a system inherited from the colonial days, when the tax laws were made for Whites. A woman was taxed according to the rate paid by her husband: it often left her very little for herself. Change. It would come, just as this first step had come, turning a woman from a child into an adult. No wonder the women in Stoddard Hall were excited. Their dancing and their movements were at least as expressive as their songs. Spilling out of the hall onto the streets, they danced all the way to the centre of the city, watched by passers-by. The expression on some of the men's faces was easy to read. Surprise. Disapproval. Yes, and fear. 'Do you not approve of women's days?' The old man's eyes looked troubled. 'Yes, one day. That is fine.' Did he think it was a celebration, like an anniversary? 'It is like Independence Day, Independence is for ever. Women's Day is also for ever.' His eyes blurred, he had not understood, did not want to understand. Mumbling in Shona, he turned away from the crowd.

Women, too, young, smartly-dressed women, stared without understanding. In a hairdressing salon, the assistant said, 'Women's Day? Why?' 'A woman is now free to decide things for herself.' Silence. Then a giggle. 'No woman is ever free. She doesn't want to be free of a man.'

Comrade Teurai Ropa Nhongo.

The women dance. They reach Parliament, in the centre of the city, and attract attention. A Minister comes out, addresses them. He shared their joy, he said, and their delight. Yet he had to remind them that *roora/lobola* still existed, and would continue to exist. True, an 18 year old could now marry without the parents' consent, but they were still entitled to *roora*. Compromise. Soothing words. Giving with one hand, withholding with the other, said a cynical bystander, a White woman. Perhaps. But for the women in front of Parliament, nothing could change the joy of that day. They had come of age. It was the first step towards women's liberation.

The struggle is only just beginning. It is bound to be a very long affair which will go on for two or three generations. I don't see that just because we have achieved political Independence, we have won. There will be a continuation of intellectual, economic and cultural liberation.

Fay Chung

Women cannot achieve change in one day. Victory will come only with long years of patience. The conflict between tradition and a law such as the Majority Act or the proposed new legislation on inheritance must continue for some time. Anomalies will continue, too. 'We must change the *lobola* system,' said Mrs Zvobgo, adding, 'But I don't mean that we must abolish it. We must change it, which will be very difficult. Parents demand *lobola* not in the same way as they used to, in the past. They behave as if they were selling their daughters. Some charge between $3,000 and $5,000! For young people this is a great deal of money. How can they pay this?'

In 1984, a judgement given by the country's Chief Justice on an aspect of the new law caused controversy. A father had sued a young man for damages because his daughter had been seduced. The Judge ruled that seduction could not have taken place, since the young woman was 20 years old and thus a consenting adult. Despite the birth of a child, therefore, the father was not awarded damages. Debate ran hot and fiery. Did this mean that the state was interfering with old customs? Did it mean that there could no longer be parental control over children? What exactly did the new law mean? Women who were outspoken, who asked for new laws on the subject of inheritance, guardianship and other aspects of family life, were ridiculed and accused of being 'women libbers'.

In November 1984, Minister Nhongo said that the law would have to be studied again to see if changes had to be made. The new law was blamed for unwanted pregnancies, 'sugar daddies', and the seduction of young women. It was argued that parents were no longer fully respected, that no government should try to dictate from the top when cultural values were involved. Clearly, this is a debate which will not and cannot be concluded hurriedly. A colloquium in November 1984, which was organised by the Ministry of Justice, Legal and Parliamentary Affairs to provide guidelines on the shape of resolutions for new legislation on the status of women, was seen by many as falling short of expectations. Learned papers, panel discussions and personal opinions were not to be faulted. The resolutions, however, once they touched *roora/lobola* or inheritance, fell short of total reform. But hope springs eternal not only in every woman's breast, but also in that of the leadership. In December 1984, Minister Zvobgo announced that a new inheritance law was being drafted.[2] Ideally, he said, half the estate should be given to the wife, half to the children. However, problems remained because of polygamy, which posed difficulties for the sharing of property.

Earlier, the Minister had said that some customs need no change. We do not believe that a child can be illegitimate, he said, adding that only a relationship between adults can be legal or illegal. He agreed, however, that some Customary laws serve to oppress women. If a woman chooses to marry under Customary law, he said, the consequences of that marriage are viewed in the courts accordingly. For example, it is presumed that under African Customary law, property is owned in common, but that is ónly how it seems on the surface. The woman never actually acquires any property except her pots and other small things. In other words, a couple may start off with nothing at all. Then, due to the hard work of both the man and the woman, they build up a nice life, a house, and acquire other immovable property during their marriage. Should there be a divorce, there is no division of property under Customary law. The woman has to leave everything to the husband. I think that this consequence of African Customary law, he said, is terribly unjust. Just think of it. Today, in modern life in urban areas, a couple can start off with only a bedroom or two and they build things up. The woman works hard, they bring up the children together — then there is a divorce, and she gets nothing. These are some of the consequences we want to look at.

Then there is the question of guardianship, he said. If a woman is married under Customary law, there is really no issue at all: the children simply belong to the husband. We want to look into that aspect and see if it is fair. Then there is inheritance. Under African Customary law, daughters don't inherit from their parents. If a man dies, his estate will devolve upon the males. The females get nothing. So we want to look at that too.

The Minister knows that the further steps will take time. The people need to be educated on the matter, because customs are tenaciously held. There must be a great deal of discussion, and meetings, too, so that the people will support this transformation. If they don't, he warned, government could march far ahead of the people and the law would not be respected. People must be asked to debate the issues. There must be a national debate on the question of *lobola*, for instance. The custom itself is excellent, but individual parents have tended to commercialise — and, therefore, to pervert — its use.

How right the Minister is on the question of 'perversion', is evident from many newspaper reports and conversations in the townships. Everyone knows of a woman who had been married to a man and then, soon after his death, returned home to find her children gone and her house stripped — that her late husband's family have exercised their traditional rights. Sometimes the woman's brother can do something, get her back at least a bed or a table. And most of the time these days, the children are left. If the husband's family live in town, they don't need them for work and would only have to feed and educate them. So the woman remains with the children and has to see how she can manage. 'It is very hard,' commented one woman sadly. 'It used to take a year, at least, before the family took over the inheritance, even the wife was not inherited before then. But now,' she added, 'you see the funeral car going to the cemetery and the family follow behind with an empty truck. They have come to collect. All the wailing and mourning with the wife is meaningless.'

In *We Carry a Heavy Load*, rural women expressed their views on various issues — *lobola*, divorce and inheritance. The *Zimbabwe Project News Bulletin* explained that the interviewers spoke in three languages with nearly 3,000 women, who were enthusiastic and anxious to give their opinions. The women ranged from their late teens to the late 70s, including young unmarried women, a majority of married women (some from polygamous households), widows and divorcees. Many were illiterate; some, especially the younger women, had had some formal education; and a few were teachers and nurses. The majority could best be described as farmer-housewives. Occasionally, group interviews were also attended by men. The formal questionnaire included such questions as: 'are you married; are you the only wife; what does being a woman mean to you; what do you think should be done to make women's lives easier? As women, what are the special difficulties you face; what do you think about husbands working away from home; do women need to earn money; do women have control over land; what are the things in the lives of women that you would like to see changed?'

The first short survey of the answers showed how clearly women understood their situation and problems. 'We carry a heavy load, being a woman' was the comment which gave the report its title. Some women felt very dejected. 'It's horrible to be a woman. All women are taken as dogs with puppies...I don't know if it's because we are created useless or we make ourselves useless and pretend to like being like that.' This comment was balanced by other remarks, such as the following: 'I am happy to be a woman. I can do more things than a man. I can sew and cook and still work in my fields just as well as any man. I feel that if I was taught to do any job that men can do, I would be able to do it.'

The women had decided ideas about property. 'I want to have equal property shares with my husband,' said one. 'There must be nobody controlling the other. I must work according to my wishes and not by force. A woman has no property at home and she has no children. When she gets divorced, she goes away naked. It is painful that even when she is working, she still owns no property of her own. Everything at home belongs to my husband. Yet I am the one who is responsible when my husband is away. We must share property and have equal right of control.'[3]

The women agree with Minister Zvobgo that they should have greater rights over their children. 'I am worried that men are said to be the children's owner,' said one, adding, 'yet I spend nine months carrying the baby in my stomach and the next 20 to 30 years looking after him or her.'

Some women feel *lobola* should be abolished. Others, however, simply want it amended, in the belief that it keeps families together. But they think that women should take part in the negotiations, particularly on the matter of the sum to be paid.

Polygamy was another issue. One woman said that she was 'treated like a child' because she was married to a polygamist. Even with the new majority status, however, all women who are married under Customary law, whether they are the first, the only, or the tenth wife, revert to the status of a child. Rudo B. Gaidzanwa, who has done research on the status of women in Zimbabwe, wrote in *The Sunday Mail* of 13 March, 1983, that women who married polygamously suffered other disabilities which were not connected with their legal status. Usually, second or third wives were much younger than the senior wife. They therefore had younger children and, unlike the older women, had no one to help them in the fields. Being younger and therefore more desirable, younger wives had another problem: being 'inherited' by the man's family. This poses a problem not mentioned in this particular article, but which a young woman — herself a member of the urban 'élite' — mentioned.

When a young woman comes into a household and the husband is much older, she is competed for by the male members of the family. Each one wants her to choose him as the heir, when her husband dies. It sounds cold but it is merely being realistic. She does have the choice. So they try to get close to her, some even trying to seduce her...and that is really terrible for a young woman. And the husband often knows what is going on. He can't take it out on his brothers, so he takes it out on the wife. He starts to beat her. There is nothing she can do. Wife-beating. That's another thing. It appears to be part of a woman's lot.

Another letter-writer to the newspapers seemed to agree, advising a woman who suffered from being beaten, to accept it on the grounds that her husband would soon tire of it — as if, with his waning strength, her lot would improve. Battered wives are not a social problem or, at least, not seen as such. One marriage counsellor (with divorce on the increase, this is an important role) advised women to be patient and to ignore their husband's absences or possible relationships outside the home. If they wanted the marriage to continue, it was argued, they should carry out their duties and remain pleasant and cheerful.

The question, of course, is whether all women *want* their marriage to continue — a question that is by no means unique to Zimbabwean society. How great are the pressures from the family and society, to be and to stay married? A woman can be single and have a child (usually the child is then brought up by the grandparents in a rural area), but there is still a tendency for single women to be seen as prostitutes. This is a legacy of the days when women in the township were in the minority and those who were single were indeed prostitutes or, at least, changed partners frequently. The ultimate pressure is economic: can the woman manage on her own? A rural woman who is divorced must leave the land from which she had obtained a living. But unless she is educated, she cannot leave. Education provides both social status and economic independence. In *We Carry A Heavy Load*, rural women said:

> Education is very important these days. Without it, we can't even read the signs on the road. We would like adult schools so that when we are taught and have knowledge, it will be easy for us to count money. Also, education will help us when we are working and speaking in co-operatives. People will be able to understand each other.

> Without education, you are nothing in this world. I wish I could be born again. I wouldn't get married so young and I would learn and learn until I die. But because it can't happen, I wish to go for adult education of any kind so that I can improve my knowledge.

All the women realised the link between education and income.

If I was educated I would be working and earning money. But because my parents didn't want to educate a daughter, I can't even help myself. Education is good due to the fact that an illiterate person will take centuries to live a better life, whereas a literate person can easily get a good job and support his or her family.

So many women are like sheep, just moving in the darkness. I say so because if you can't read or write you're just like a dead body staying with people. If old women are taught to have some sort of knowledge they will act as young women, because of that knowledge.

Some men oppose the idea of education for their wives, even preventing their women from joining agricultural extension classes. Women think it's because men don't want their women to come into contact with other men. Also, the heavy workload and consequent lack of energy prevents rural women from attending classes regularly. Thus, while the first step has been taken to change the legal status of women, or at least of those who are unmarried, a number of further steps must follow. What is encouraging is that the leaders are acutely aware of the need to transform society.

Baby Dumping

The concept of 'baby dumping' entered the political and social scene in Zimbabwe some three years after Independence. In August 1983, Prime Minister Robert Mugabe spoke about it at a rally marking National Youth Day. He thundered against the practice of baby dumping which, he said, had become a new phenomenon, especially in urban areas, the 'high density' suburbs and the former 'locations'. Young women who became pregnant and were unable to arrange an abortion, furtively 'dumped' the unwanted infant after birth. Public toilets, school facilities, drains, streams, and shallow ditches became the depositories of baby bodies. Official figures placed the rate of dumped babies at one a week. Unofficially, it was believed greatly to exceed this figure.

The young mothers were reviled. Following the Prime Minister's remarks, a Cabinet Committee was formed to investigate the problem. The letters page in the Harare daily, *The Herald*, was filled with comments on the subject. Women unfortunate enough to be traced, were given tough prison sentences. There were radio programmes and denunciations, but little analysis. Some social workers mumbled that Depo Provera, the injected contraceptive, should be freely available. They acknowledged that Depo Provera had adverse side effects, but advocated it on the grounds that it was easy. Oral contraceptives, the loop and other methods, are difficult to come by for women who are insecure and who know that their husbands would like to have many children. 'A woman who is barren is as useless as a woman who is lazy,' explained a social worker. 'Don't forget, women were married for their services and their womb. It is difficult to change such ideas overnight. What has also not changed is the relationship between the sexes. The woman is submissive, the man demanding. The problem is that today's women, particularly young women, are easily accessible. They go to the same schools as boys and often, fellow students and teachers are responsible for the unwanted pregnancies of schoolgirls. Then there is the problem of sudden wealth. The young girls — yes, some are schoolgirls — are mad about clothes, radios, what they think are the good things in life. There are only too many old men prepared to offer them these things now. You can see these girls hanging about the hotels. Usually their parents have no idea how their daughters spend their time after school. It seems so easy. Until they fall pregnant.'

Not all pregnancies which end in baby dumping are those of schoolgirls. One case reported in court is typical of others. A young servant girl in a small country town, who earned even less than the prescribed minimum wage, fell pregnant. The father, an unemployed labourer, was in no position to marry the girl or support the child. Afraid of losing her job, she carried the newborn baby to the river, which became its grave. The mother was traced after the body was found, because the employers, who had known of the pregnancy, reported her to the authorities.

Economic pressures and social constraints are the major causes of baby dumping, said Kumbirai Kangai, a member of the Cabinet Committee, when he was the Minister of Labour and Social Services. He called on women in trouble to report to his Ministry for help, instead of dumping their babies. But how many women knew of the offer, and how many would be able to keep their babies and their jobs? Schoolgirls know that pregnancies end their schooldays and, with that, any prospects of a career. 'We want education with production, not reproduction,' said the Minister of Education and Culture, Dr Dzingai Mutumbuka, horrified that during 1982, more than 1,300 schoolgirls had become mothers.

'Women alone are blamed, they alone carry the stigma. Men should be made to share the burden,' said one social worker. A law that applied to both married and unmarried fathers was passed, which compelled them to maintain their offspring. However, court orders alone cannot and do not compel men to fulfil their obligations. 'Not in a society where women are very much the second persons,' maintained the social worker. 'Society must change. It is changing. We are in a state of change, you know that. Government does its best. There is the new law about majority, the law about maintenance, minimum wages and so on. But it is not enough. The attitudes of people must change.'

One thousand women came to a meeting on the subject that was called by Comrade Sally Mugabe. Ideas were tossed about. Most women felt that sex education and counselling were important. There was a feeling, too, that financial problems might well be the primary cause. It was difficult to find solutions, given the economic constraints of an economy suffering from the world recession and a two-year-old drought. 'Women always have a fall-back position,' said one social worker, sadly. 'They turn to prostitution in times of strain. If there are only roots, wild berries and grass to eat for your children, what do you do? Go to the urban areas and sell yourself.'

It was this 'fall-back position' which led to an alarming operation in late October, 1983. The police, army, and eventually even the ruling ZANU Party's Youth Brigade, swooped on women, six thousand in all, and dragged them off to prison cells on suspicion of being prostitutes. The operation was coupled with a swoop on squatters, the people who had left the rural areas and were living in squalid make-shift housing at the edge of the cities. Some squatters were too close to dams and rivers, polluting scarce water supplies, while others were living on mission or private farm land. Rumours were rife that squatter camps were the vice dens of criminals and beggars.

In Harare, the red light district was seen to have moved from a slum area at the edge of the city centre, to the centre itself. The 'avenues', flats adjoining the business centre, had acquired an army of pretty Black girls employed in the capital's offices and shops. Some prostitutes had moved in along with other single women, just as call girls were now freely entering the city hotels, which were no longer the preserve of Whites. It was also a new development that men, single and married, hunted in packs for women. In a country where polygamy is not outlawed either by custom or law, mistresses have become status symbols, just like good jobs and large cars. It was neither unjustified nor inexplicable, therefore, that the government became worried. What *was* unexpected, was the scale of the operation and the form that it took.

The first report to give details of the initial swoop made it clear that the action had been carried out under the cover of darkness. Following this event, *The Herald* was almost coy in the manner of its coverage. Anyone with access to the overseas media was better informed about women being arrested as they walked in the streets, about women being held for days while they were 'checked out', having to prove the existence of a family, a job, or both. Similar actions followed elsewhere in the country. The tourist centres were combed for single women, but *The Herald* gave more prominence to ministers' speeches than to 'Operation Cleanup'. Rumours ebbed and flowed: it was said that

A workshop organised by the women's action group, Women Speak Out, which was set up to focus attention on the oppression of women.

women were being sent to the Zambezi Valley; that they were being raped, that women were unable to inform their families of their arrest, and that they had been forced to leave children on their own when they were picked up. Fear swept the high density areas. Women no longer went out. Police, swooping on an area, used Youth Brigade informers to tell them of single women allegedly plying their 'trade'.

Only the readers' letters to the paper gave an inkling of events and people's reactions. A Women's Action Group was formed, mainly by intellectuals, both Black and White. It called on the Minister of Community Development and Women's Affairs to take action, sought an interview with the Prime Minister, and began to organise a seminar on prostitution. By this time, the seething reaction had forced the authorities not only to address the issue in the House of Assembly (where it was established that 6,300 women had been arrested), but also to release the women. It transpired that most of them had been sent to a desolate camp in the hot and dry Zambezi Valley. The area was known as the Mushumbi Pools, but the romantic name was not matched by the corrugated pre-fab huts or the terrible conditions that were being suffered by the women.

The media hailed the government's action in releasing the women as magnanimous. A Cabinet Minister acknowledged privately that the affair had been mishandled, but added that respectable women had supported Operation Cleanup. Some readers of *The Herald*, indeed, wrote letters expressing their jubilation that the 'professionals' would be unable to lay their hands on men's Christmas bonuses, which would instead be spent on the legal families. What had gone wrong, the Minister thought, was the over-enthusiasm of the police, who had arrested women at random. He would not be drawn on allegations of abuse or the suggestion that 'real' prostitutes had been given the tip-off about the operation to come and had lain low — that the majority of the detained women were housewives, secretaries, or simply unemployed women.

The reaction was strong. Marriages broke up, with husbands refusing to believe that their wives had been picked up simply 'on suspicion', and jobs were lost. Social stigma was attached by some to the arrested women. Women learnt to walk in fear. The Women's Action Group spoke of 'anti-women reactions', and letters to the newspaper demanded to know whether it was now legally required for a woman to carry a marriage licence in her handbag or some proof of employment, much as Blacks in South Africa have to carry pass books. There were few answers to many questions. Why were men not penalised for using prostitutes? There is no law against prostitution, only against soliciting. Yet the women were not picked up for soliciting. In fact, the Emergency Powers had been used to hold them as detainees.

Abhorrence over baby dumping may have started it all, but male insecurity must also have been responsible. Male dominance had been challenged in Zimbabwe since Independence. Women who carried the gun during the war had demanded emancipation after it: equal training and equal job opportunities. The old image of the subdued woman appeared to be disappearing. Men, ill at ease in any case at the swift pace of change, reacted too strongly. When women were suddenly helpless and, thanks to a directive from the highest level, at their mercy, they lost their perspective, their common sense and the respect they had been taught to show to women. When it was all over, sanity seemed to return. The veil of secrecy which foreigners had failed to penetrate, was possibly beneficial. Society could lick its wounds, heal rifts, and start again.

Footnotes:

1. *The Herald*, 7 December 1984.

2. *The Herald*, 7 December 1984.

3. In January 1986, the Matrimonial Causes Act was passed, which provides for property to be divided between husband and wife in the event of their divorce. However this is more likely to benefit middle class women who have greater access to legal facilities.
    A Succession Bill to protect a widow from being disposesed by her in-laws is also being debated.

All over Zimbabwe, parents are helping to build schools for their children, they even make the bricks. Nyadzonya School, which is pictured above, was named after the raid on Nyadzonya Camp in Mozambique during the struggle.

6

PERIOD OF CHANGE

In Harare, the heady atmosphere of politics tends to obscure what the people in the rural areas, slowly coming to grips with Independence, do and feel. But it is evident that the people are motivated by the new freedom to work hard for a better life. Minister Teurai Ropa Nhongo once said that she was distressed because rural women had said: 'Independence is only for the educated.' She was, and still is, determined to change all that, to ensure education for all, even for the old and illiterate.

If women thought that Independence was only for the educated, that only the educated woman could earn money, free herself of subservience to the male in her household, then they were wrong, she said. For women are no longer confined to the home, but are attending the women's clubs, which engage in traditional female pursuits, such as sewing, knitting, crocheting, home-crafts and home economics. They enjoy it, they learn, they work — and they want more.

Throughout *We Carry a Heavy Load*, runs the theme: 'We want to participate in making decisions'. Women now want to talk at meetings. They know their young daughters spoke at huge rallies in the Mozambique camps and they no longer want to be kept in the background. They object to the phrase, 'you talk like a woman', which is used by men to abuse each other. Women want not only to lead women and to implement women's rights, but also to sit on local councils and vote more women into Parliament.

'Women are very active, there are so many women's organisations, such as the Women's Institute, those in the villages, the Churches and of course the Parties — women are on the march,' said one woman leader. She wanted to remain unnamed because she added the following controversial rider:

> Women have moved away from demanding equal rights: they want more rights than men, because they think they are the people who keep agriculture going in the rural area — they want to own the land. Wouldn't you, if you worked on it, day after day? They are not even sure about communal ownership — nor about co-operative ownership. It's their sweat and blood that's mixed into that soil, so they want it legally. If the husband is away, he has no duties to perform. And he doesn't work the land! Why should he have the right to decide on the crops, on their disposal — and eventually, when he dies, why should *his* family have the land?

Kate Truscott

Women and men working together in the Wedza Communal Land. The weir they are building will provide irrigation for their garden project.

It may not be right, but so far it is the custom. Women leaders urge women to become self-confident, to speak their minds, to ensure that they are respected, and that their status depends on themselves and their own efforts in the community, not on the fact that they have a husband.

Land: this is a major issue. Land means so much more to women who have no hope of working in the cash sector. The land resettlement schemes attract the women who yearn to leave the over-used communal lands. Control: this is what they want, the right to decide everything concerning the land on which they work. No, independence is not only for the educated. The peasant woman may move slowly, she may not always speak her mind, but she does know her mind — and, in time, she and her daughters will reach their goal.

'All my children go to school now,' said a tall woman, pausing to pile up stones at the edge of her garden. 'I must work myself. The extended family system is finished. We are no longer together. I work alone. This is my land. I will fight to keep it, even when my husband goes. The old barter system — work-for-beer, the *nhimbe* — no longer functions. We need money for fertiliser, for seeds — for those things co-operatives are good; if we have these things we can grow more and don't have to buy mealie meal.'

It is a common demand: women must help themselves, say the leaders. Women *are* helping themselves, as experience has shown. There is tremendous energy, tremendous motivation out in the rural areas. Women are so keen to learn. They crowd around the mobile clinics, they are keen to use a special Zimbabwean invention, a simple ventilated toilet, which traps flies in a pipe that also serves to keep the stench down. A small thing? Not when the lack of sanitary facilities has for so long been a source of sickness. Children are brought for vaccination, women listen to advice on child-spacing, urging that men, too, are involved. Nothing, after all, will change without both men and women pulling at the same end of the rope, as one old woman put it.

Driving at night along the well-tarred main roads (another legacy of war) can be misleading. The clear sky, the stillness of the bush, the night noises of the crickets at song are deceptive: it seems as if the bush is still and at peace. There *is* peace, but there is also a clamour for change, which is not to be subdued.

Everyone is keen on change. Sometimes it happens too quickly. Look at our school children: 800,000 or so in school in 1979; by 1983, more than two and a half million. Sounds great. But is it? Where will they go, these educated children? In the past, they stayed on the land. Now, with some school certificate, they want a desk job. Who can give them that?

It is a complaint one often hears. Complaint may be the wrong word: perhaps concern is more appropriate. After Independence, it all seemed there for the taking: education, health services, better jobs. Education opened the doors to knowledge but not necessarily to a cash job. Previously, the privileges and opportunities had been restricted to a quarter of a million people. But suddenly, they had to be distributed between seven million. Dorothy, an ex-combatant, described herself as a realist.

> It is natural, people have waited so long for this. They don't understand why their lives didn't change overnight, why it can't change overnight. Change should be gentle. If there had been no war, if we had gone through the same thing as, say Zambia, the expectation wouldn't be so high, the disappointment not so great.

There is disappointment, there had to be disappointment, insisted Dorothy.

> Take me. I was in the war. I came back and had to return to school, to do 'O' levels. Otherwise, I couldn't find a job. My war experience didn't count. I'm one of the lucky ones, I passed my five 'O' levels and now I'm taking 'A's, and I know how to type. I share a house with other ex-combatants and I enjoy life.
> But take my mother — she doesn't understand me. At first she was proud, she still is proud, that I was a soldier. But I don't go home often, I don't like it when I see how the women in the village go down on their knees to offer food to the men. An older woman I know performs these duties when she visits her husband's village. She says, we must build a bridge between those who were in the struggle and the older people, between the urban and the rural areas. We are the same people. We *are* the same people, that is true, but the rate of change is different. Take the children: they go to school now, but they don't learn the things they used to. Do you know that there were thousands of pregnancies last year? Among schoolchildren? You see, although the old system is breaking up, there are things left over. In the past, no parent spoke to the children directly about sex. That was the job of the aunts and uncles. Now the family consists only of parents and children, while the aunts and uncles are somewhere else. But they can't break the custom, the taboo. So no one tells them anything. When I become a teacher, I'll fight for sex education.

Dorothy is 24 years old, bright and cheerful. She is confident that, given time and goodwill, all these problems can be solved. She shares this optimism with others, including the leaders.

Sex is very difficult in a society in transformation. Now with the drought, many women sell themselves — it's all they have to sell. Also, many divorced women have no other way. We have abortion, legal abortion, but it's very difficult to get the agreement of doctors. I saw a film on television that said the so-called miscarriages — the result of attempted abortion — had gone up by 10% each year since 1979. Usually the women involved are young girls. Many girls die...they never reach hospital or they die in hospital. Others can never have children again.

What we must do is accept that these things are happening. We women must take a lead. We must fight for family planning, we must see to it that men change their views about it. It's called child-spacing now, and there are some mobile clinics that go around — but it isn't enough. My worst worry is the men: they still want many children and quiet wives. My brother, for example, wants a traditional wife, one who won't disagree with him. I argue. He thinks that's terrible. We must try to talk about these things: pregnancies, abortion, family planning. That's as important as nutrition and hygiene. No, it's part of it.

Some White radicals wanted to open a rape centre. But no Black women supported this. Rape happens, oh yes. It happened during the war, it often happened then. But this is another taboo. When something like this happens to a woman, she wants no one to know except her family. She goes back to the family for security and shelter. I don't believe this will change for a long time.

There has been positive change: women can now claim maternity leave from work. They can even take a man to court to pay for a child. Who knows, maybe we'll be able to change the man's attitude of 'a child a year'.

Legislation is fine. But change, real change, can only come if attitudes change — on the part of both men and women, the leaders and the people.

Co-operatives

Near Harare's airport is a sign which says, Simukai Farm Co-operative. 'Simukai,' says the friendly guide, 'means stand up.' And that is what the members of the co-operative want to do. They want to stand proudly and independently.

Margaret Waller

An ex-ZIPRA combatant works on the Simukai Farm Co-operative near Harare.

No one seems to be about. A cock crows, chickens cluck. A man walks up to the car, unsmiling. Then he recognises the guide and nods. We are welcome, after all. Suspicion is understandable. Because this co-operative is so close to the centre of Harare, because it is one of the many supported by the Zimbabwe Project, and because it is composed of former freedom fighters, it is a popular spot for political tourists.

Women? We were interested in women? Very well. But we would have to wait. Everyone was busy. Also, there was a meeting of the committee, of which several members were women.

A White man still owns the farm, our guide explains. The co-operative is renting it. But the members have organised the piggery, the chicken farm and the vegetable gardens. We walk around, noticing an old borehole. Then we see a new one nearby, built by the members. Finally, they come. First a woman who works with the pigs, wearing gum boots and sturdy clothing. Others come. We gather in what had once been a storeroom, huddling together on wooden benches so that everyone can listen, while members of the 60-strong co-operative speak. All of them are former combatants and the majority are women. Only one old woman sits a little apart quietly listening, not following the English. She had been on the farm before, but had stayed on and joined them.

Talent Nyathi, a 22-year-old mother of two small children, explains:

> Many of us were in camps in Zambia. In ZIPRA camps. This means we have many people who come from Matabeleland. But there is no trouble between those who are Ndebele and those who are Shona. Not in a co-operative like this. We are one people. That's how it was in the war.

> Our women members feel equal to men. There is no discrimination. Women work in all departments, as you can see. The secretary of the co-operative is a woman and our finances are looked after by a woman. Only four members are married. One woman's husband, who works outside, is not a member. No one leaves the farm when they marry. There is no need. The co-operative is not only a way of life, it's a job — for life.

> Some of the comrades lost their own men in the war. Some have children they must look after. Myself? Well, I was in a school near the border with Botswana. We decided to cross the border. We all went, teachers and students. At first, we didn't really know what would happen. In Botswana, everyone was very excited. It was the first time a whole school had arrived like that. The journey had been tough and suddenly there were all these people, even

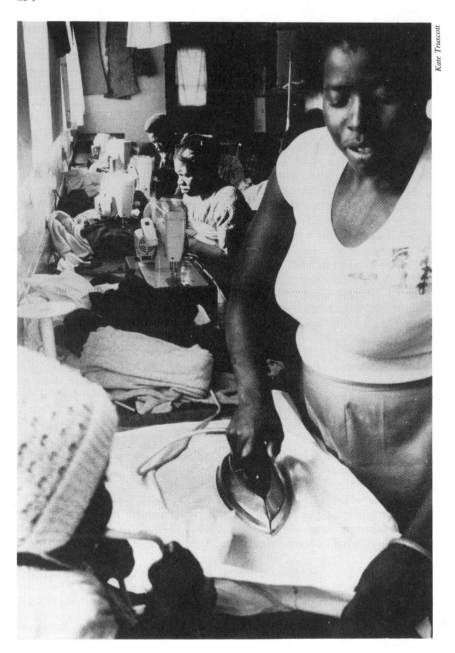

Kate Truscott

A co-operative of women ex-combatants in Wedza, which sews and sells school uniforms and clothes.

journalists. Everyone wanted to know if we had come on our own or been forced. Our parents came and asked the same thing. But only a few children went back with the parents. A few weeks later, we were flown to Zambia on a Hercules aircraft.

We are different from women who were not in the struggle. We are responsible. We can do things for ourselves. If we marry, we know that there is no need to pay *lobola*. But we do it, because we don't want to hurt our parents. Some parents are changing too. Some fathers say, let us keep the custom, but let them give me a small gift. After all, I am not selling my daughter.

There are other co-operatives. The co-operative magazine *Vanguard*, wrote a report in its July 1982 issue on the Kusimudzira Co-operative in Mutare, a group of six former combatants who had attended a six-month course at Melfort, near Harare. The Ministry of Community Development and Women's Affairs helped to pay the fees and the upkeep of the students. They had hoped to produce dyed cloth in the style of West African material. All the items produced during the course were sold quickly. The students then moved to Mutare, where they set up their co-operative, which was financed by the Zimbabwe Project. Their main problem was the shortage of suitable dyes, which had to be imported.

The same issue also reported the progress of a co-operative in Wedza, which had 20 former female freedom fighters as members. They, too, had taken a course at Melfort, from October 1981 to March 1982, supported by the National Women's Organisation. When the women discussed what they would do at the end of the course, they realised that despite their new skills (they were learning sewing), there would be little chance of being employed in the private sector. A co-operative seemed the only answer. Fortunately, they had heard through the Zimbabwe Project that their project would be welcomed at a mission station in Wedza. Everyone was very supportive and helped them to build a workroom, tables and chairs, as well as to obtain machines and material.

The women moved in on April 23 and began tackling work in their little factory. They were making school uniforms, for which there was a huge demand.

I am a housewife, but I am also head of the family. So I don't see any difference between a man and a woman. I can do any kind of work which must be done by my husband. I feel I am a very important person and I would like other women to know that men are not everything. I say, thank goodness I am born a woman.

Collective Action

'Listen, Mpiri,' said an old woman, her toothless mouth opening sternly. The woman stirring the huge pot of sadza stopped for a moment, as she was spoken to. From a nearby hut came the wailing of children. 'They are sick, those children. All day, all night, they cry.' The younger woman went on with the work. Yes, there was trouble. Mrs Chinamora, the children's mother and the wife of a relative, had no land. She lived in the village but could only work when someone gave her something to do. Her husband, Elias, who worked in the town, sent her money. Only sometimes, there wasn't any money. Like now. That was why the children cried. 'Mpiri. When we have eaten, you visit them.' The old woman nodded. The muscles on her neck had slackened, so she nodded even when she wanted to shake her head. Her name was Martha and she was greatly respected in the village — even the n'anga had been known to seek her advice. 'Take the sadza, there will be enough.'

When Mpiri returned, she had to repeat everything she had seen and heard. Two months ago, she told Martha, Elias Chinamora had visited his family. He became angry because his wife was not feeding their one year old child. When she said there was nothing left for her, he beat her. Since then, there had been no milk for the baby. The money had not come since he had left. Did the child eat? Mpiri said that the child had eaten, but that there were no groundnuts and no milk in the hut. Not even mats. Mrs Chinamora had sold her last mats to buy some sadza. Both children were thin, said Mpiri, and the young one had something dripping from her eyes and nose.

In the morning, Mpiri was sent over again, with milk. She returned at once and said the child had vomited after the sadza and had been sick all night. The old woman was anxious and sent Mpiri to tell Mrs Chinamora to go at once to the hospital. She herself, she said, would provide the money for the bus fare. It was time to get ready, because the bus would soon arrive. Mpiri admired Martha, her mother-in-law, because she was wise and good and knew so much. She patiently answered all her questions about the child: the colour of the vomit, the frequency of the spasms, whether she also had diarrhoea and whether her stomach was swollen.

When Mpiri returned from the bus stop (she had carried the older child on her back), she asked, 'Will the child die, my mother?' 'It is for the ancestors to decide.' She was silent all day, chewing tobacco, sitting in front of the hut and looking down towards the path which led to the bus stop. Mbuya Martha loved all the children in the village. She knew exactly who and what they were: Gideon, a shy little boy whom she called her 'politician'; Mpiri's children, Tandi and Samanga, both already in grade one, quiet, clever and her own grandchildren; Jacob, who loved snakes; and Kamba, who hated them and was afraid when he went out with the herd. She knew these and the others and they all came to her with their little stories. Would the child die? She should have visited her before. But Mrs Chinamora was proud. She could not afford to join the Women's Club, though once they had visited her and had advised her to put aside five cents a week, so that she should have some money saved for the bus and other special things. She had shaken her head and said that when her money came, it was only just enough to buy food.

Martha walked through the village, to the background of constant greetings and the cry of children's voices. She wanted to see the n'anga, who lived at the foot of the hill. But before she got to the footpath, she came back — no one should interfere between a man and his wife. It was not right. It was true that Mrs Chinamora was family, because Elias Chinamora, like most of the people in the village, was a relation. But she, Martha, was a woman, not a man. She must respect the custom. When she returned to the place where she had sat and chewed tobacco, Mpiri told her that the child was in the hospital. Mrs Chinamora was there also, according to someone who had been on the bus. The child would die. Mbuya Martha had seen many children die like this. Bad food, the nurses said — not enough, and the wrong food. But where could they get better food? The men wanted maize in their fields, not vegetables. Mrs Chinamora had no land, so her food was bought from other families, from the shop near the bus stop.

The child died three days later. Mrs Chinamora came back with the older child and for three days they sat and mourned. Elias Chinamora came, too, and beat his wife because his child was dead. That was in the morning of the day on which the Women's Club was scheduled to meet. Martha walked past Elias. She had mourned with him, waiting for his child. Now she stood and looked at him. He was a big man, his shirt hanging over his trousers and his breath came to her as she faced him under the baobab tree near the Women's Club, a small hut they had built soon after Independence. He greeted her and she responded. He was bereaved. But he was also the one who had killed the child. The spirits were angry. So she spoke, softly, through her toothless mouth. 'The child was sick with hunger. You have a job in town. Your wife should be there. Here there is nothing for her.'

He was sullen like a whipped dog. No woman had spoken to him in this manner since he had been a child. 'She has a house. I send money.'

'No. It is not enough. She must be in town. Or you must find land.' He knew what she meant — that there were new places where the government sent people who had no land. But Elias did not want to live in the rural areas. He liked the town life, he liked the beer and,

Kate Truscott

A meeting of the Women's Club in Bohera (Sabi Communal Land). The woman in the foreground is making a blanket from tree bark; the others are making table mats.

sometimes, he liked to enjoy another woman. 'This is my home.'

'There is no field for you.' It was true. There was no more land. All the women had come and they stood and looked. Elias knew they were there. He wanted to walk on, but his legs felt weak.

'You are going to the bus?'

He shook his head. He was planning to go, he said, but not immediately. The old woman and her friends frightened him, and he remembered the screams of his wife in the night. 'I'll go tomorrow.'

Martha nodded her head. He *would* go tomorrow. And he would take his wife, she was sure of that. He would be afraid that she had bewitched him, that his other child would also die. He had a job. If his wife were clever, she could get the money when he was paid. She could also sell things herself. Mats, pots. There were many people in the town who needed things like that. Here, in the village, everyone could make mats and pots.

Elias walked back to his hut. The eyes of the women followed him and they waited until he had gone. They had helped. Martha knew that without them, she could not have spoken as she did, could not have shamed him as she knew she had done. A few weeks ago, there had been a visitor to the Women's Club. She had spoken of many things. Collective action, she had explained, was best: women should learn knitting together, learn to write and read together, start a vegetable garden together. Perhaps she was right. Meanwhile, there had already been some collective action. It was time to start the meeting.

'The Secret'

The story that follows partly deals with the question of polygamy. Polygamy is legal in Zimbabwe, as a glance at the marriage bans posted outside any District Administrator's office proves: 'Rosemary Banda, spinster...John Dhlamini, polygamist...', is a typical description of people proposing to marry.

Polygamy is a problem for some women. Now that society has changed, a new wife often no longer serves the interests of senior wives in terms of labour. The young wife is an irritant, and sometimes also a source of jealousy, because she pleases the husband most. An editorial in *The Herald* (10 December, 1984) declared that: 'Polygamy is loathed by most Zimbabweans as an outmoded practice which enslaves and oppresses women. We say it is a cancer and it is time legislators helped to discourage it by passing laws which are heavily loaded against polygamous marriages.'

'The Secret', however, is really about impotency. Many men dislike accepting that they are responsible for childlessness. It is the woman who is blamed. And a barren woman has no future: she is sent home in disgrace to her parents, who must return the *lobola/roora* payment. Some women, therefore, resort to desperate measures to ensure progeny.

Independence climbed slowly to the top of the huge rock which balanced on two huge slabs of granite jutting out of the ground. Similar formations were scattered all over the bush, but she had chosen this one because it was the largest. She needed to be away from everything — the work, the people, even the ground. She glanced down towards her bicycle, which she had leant against the clump of thornbush trees below.

Yes, she needed to be alone. It was not the first time she had gone off on her own to work out a problem. She was used to problems, ever since she had joined the struggle: immediately after Form III, she had actually led a group of four across the border, even though she was a girl. Then everything had followed so very quickly: the training camp, some months in an operational area, advanced training in Tanzania and then the study trip to Yugoslavia. That is where she had decided to become a doctor. She had wanted to stay and complete her schooling, so that she could enter university, but it had not worked out like that.

She did not mind now, since she was doing the kind of work she had hoped to do then — being with the people, teaching them, while learning herself. She was still young, 23 years old, and sometime would be able to fulfil the rest of her ambitions. Now she was a medical assistant in this area. Once they had called it a 'purchase area', a region where Blacks could buy small farms. It was worth it, all this hard work. But hard work would not solve the problem with Zachariah Chipembe; it was not simply a health problem. She crossed her hands behind her neck and gazed across the valley, which was dotted with patches of cotton fields. There were fields of cotton, maize, cassava and groundnuts. This was a fairly well-off region.

Zachariah Chipembe was a farmer who had every right to be proud of his property and of what he had achieved. He was a 'master farmer', and lived in a brick house. He also had two wives and three children. In fact, he had three wives: it was almost a year since he had paid *roora* for his third wife, Tima. She was the reason for Independence's decision to climb up onto the rocks and think. She was worried about Tima. The young woman had thrown herself on the ground, weeping, because after almost a year, she was still not pregnant. She was still as flat as she had been on her wedding night. Zachariah had beaten her, once very badly. She wanted a child so much. 'Why were the ancestors angry?' she had asked, moaning.

So Independence had sent her to town. The test results had been absolutely clear. There was no reason whatsoever why Tima should not have a child. She was healthy and everything functioned as it should. Tima could have children — just as Mary had borne Zachariah two daughters and Betty had borne him a son. Tima. Poor little Tima. Seventeen years old and so unhappy. It was so very important for a woman to prove she was a woman by bearing children. Independence sighed again. It was hard to discuss problems with men like Zachariah. But it was the custom to have children and it was important for Tima to bear a child.

Independence made up her mind. She jumped lightly down and took her bicycle. She would have to talk to Zachariah's wives. Both were respected in the area and were leading members of the Women's Club. Mary, the oldest, had married when she and Zachariah were both very young. Independence passed Mary's garden and admired the care with which everything had been tended. Mary was a hard worker and she also had Hope, her younger daughter, to help her. Charity, the older daughter, was married and had children of her own.

Independence halted. She had spotted Mary with her hoe slung over her shoulder, preparing to leave the field. 'Good morning, Amai Hope,' said Independence, softly clapping her hands and bowing correctly. She had learnt that it was easier to work with the people if she accepted the old customs. 'Good morning. I am well, if you are well.' They faced each other. The older woman was thin and tall, like her own beans, with her breasts sagging beneath the dress. The younger woman was in the prime of life.

'Two weeks ago I went to town with Comrade Master Farmer,' she said casually. 'For me it was great, I enjoyed seeing some of my comrades again.' That had not been the reason for the trip. She had been able to persuade Zachariah to go with her to the hospital for an examination. She added quickly, before Mary could react: 'My father works in town. He was glad to see the child.' Independence was respected not only because she had been a combatant, was educated and worked in the clinic, but also because she had a child. 'Men think it is important to have children, don't you think so, Amai?' Another woman joined them, a woman who was as stout as Mary was thin, who spoke as loudly as Mary spoke softly. This was Betty, Zachariah's second wife, mother of his son, Pearce.

Betty must have heard their voices, for her garden was nearby. The greetings began, the polite exchange of words, which seemed to Independence to cover a good deal — fear, jealousy? Perhaps even hate? In town, Zachariah had bought gifts for his wives, the mothers of his children. For Tima, he had bought a small mirror and had frowned when he showed it to Independence. He had remembered that he had been married for almost a year to Tima and she had still not fallen pregnant. Perhaps she did not deserve even a mirror. But how could she possibly have a child? The doctor's verdict had been quite clear. Never, not once, could Zachariah have fathered a child. Any child. The tests had been conclusive. Yet there stood Mary and Betty, the mothers of Zachariah's son and daughters, facing her.

'How is Pearce?' Independence asked Betty. Pearce. An odd name. There was no White farmer in the district by that name. Betty had never been to school, yet she had named her son Pearce. They walked. Independence looked over her shoulder at Betty. 'I was only a little girl when the British sent Lord Pearce here,' she said. 'I was already at school. I remember when the Pearce Commission came.' She was walking ahead, aware that the women followed, one treading close on the heels of the other. Had she turned she would have seen how serious they were.

She walked on, speaking lightly about those days in 1971. 'I was at home when some comrades came and told us to say "no" if Pearce asked what we thought of the British proposals. No! And that's what happened everywhere, didn't it.' She felt the silence, sensed the hostility, behind her. Independence turned and said, 'We're near the clinic. Would you like to join me in some tea?' They nodded and followed the younger woman inside.

'Yes.' Independence took up the theme again. 'I remember it well, the Pearce Commission. The reason was that I did well in my exams that week and was so excited. One remembers occasions for such silly reasons. I remember, too, the men and women dancing all night.' She had invented this tale on the spur of the moment. In fact, she had no idea if it was exam time when Pearce had been on his rounds. Pearce was something she had heard about, not experienced. Ian Smith had worked out something with the British and they had come to explain it to the people and ask their opinion. The liberation movements had wanted none of it. They wanted Independence and majority rule, so everyone had to say 'no'.

It was Mary who spoke first. 'I remember it. There was a beer drinking party. We brewed beer, all of us. People came and said we must say 'no'. She added proudly, 'Zachariah was on the committee. He helped to write the big placards which we held up when they came. In the evening after they had gone, we danced again.'

Of course, Independence agreed silently. That's how it had happened: a beer festival. Zachariah, proud of his participation, would no doubt have been drinking, and Mary could have made sure that he drank plenty. At night, it would have been easy to slip away from a party in a village. And there were many places in the bush which could hide secrets — such as a man lying next to a woman, without the man being quite sure who she was, especially if he was drunk and she sober.

Charity — Hope — good names for girls. And then Pearce, who was 10 years old. It was just about 10 years and what — nine months? — since Lord Pearce and the other Commissioners had visited this Purchase Land Area. 'It is hard if a woman has no children,' said Independence, pouring the tea. 'My mother told me that if a woman had no children, she was not alive. It was as if she had never been born.'

Neither woman spoke. Nor did they drink their hot tea. Independence continued. 'Even today, some things have not yet changed. It is still important for a woman to have a child. We women know this. Just as we know that it isn't always the fault of the woman who has no child. It can be the fault of the man. But he doesn't know and in any case, he will not believe it. What can the woman do? Her father won't like it. He would not return the *roora*, so where could she go? Stay with a man who can't give her a child and who abuses her because of that? Even if it *is* his fault? It is hard sometimes to be a woman.' Betty, the younger wife, the mother of Pearce, replied. 'Women are needed to work and to have children. Children also work for the family. We all work. On a farm like this, there is plenty of work.' Independence cried eagerly, 'Of course there is! That must have been one reason why Zachariah brought home a young wife — to help on the farm after Charity had gone away.' Betty said reluctantly: 'We manage, we know how to work. We too can drive a tractor, like Zachariah. When we need help with the crops we can pay. Widows get a dollar a day.'

Independence was sure of her ground now. They both knew, had known for a long time, that Zachariah was impotent. They had shared the secret with each other, but not with the young Tima. They didn't need her. They were jealous of her youthful vitality. Independence went on. 'Yes, things change all the time. One of these days, even the widows will be well looked after. The Women's Clubs are working so hard to show people how to earn money — sewing clothes, making pots, selling things. They won't work always for a dollar a day. Everything is getting expensive.'

Silence. They knew Independence was right. They had paid more last week for tea and washing powder than ever before. 'Besides,' Independence smiled, 'it's nice for everyone if there is a child in a family. Everyone is happy. Especially the father.' Independence remembered how quiet, not to say bad-tempered, Zachariah had been. What was he like at home? Worse, naturally. She picked up the cups, which had not been touched. 'Next week is the anniversary of Independence. I'm very much looking forward to it. I met so many comrades in town and they want to come here to visit me. I said, yes, this is a good time, everyone will be happy! Perhaps the Women's Club

Here women show their commitment to the continuing struggle for women's rights. This picture was taken outside Parliament on 10 December, 1982, when the Legal Age of Majority Act was passed.

can organise a dance, too — they are combatants, soldiers, perhaps they will perform some of their physical exercises as part of the celebrations. Of course you are members of the Club. I don't know if you can help?' The women got up. First Mary, then Betty. Mary spoke in her thin old woman's voice, without looking at the younger woman. 'We will help. Yes. We will speak to the other members.' They clapped their hands. Independence responded, subservient to the older women. 'It is true,' Mary went on, 'children are very important for everyone. The celebrations will be well organised. Tima can help, too — if that is all right.' Independence, still clasping her hands and curtseying, asked, 'Tima is a member of the Women's Club?' 'She can join,' said both women, almost speaking as one.

The Future: Hope

No woman should be suppressed only because she is a woman, just as it is wrong to oppress someone just because he or she is Black.

Jane Ngwenya

An ex-combatant wrote:

I read in *Moto* magazine that 25 years ago, people already knew that genuine liberation depended on two things — good housing and women's education. Africans lacked a calm home background and their mothers were illiterate. Africans needed educated wives and educated mothers for their families.

It is a pity that it's taken so long to see things that way. Really, we're only at the beginning. The third struggle is the struggle for our own culture and against customs which are no longer valid. It is not a struggle against men, just as the second struggle was not against Whites. We fought a system then and we fight a system now. The third struggle must give the woman equality, but should not oppress the man.

Women on the land must be recognised for what they do: the production of food. In the urban areas, working women must insist that their husbands share the household duties. The daughter must struggle for her mother and must work to bring clinics, transport and cinemas to the rural areas. Women need some fun — not only work. A woman must struggle to understand that fewer children mean happier wives and healthier children.

Childen, too, must struggle to understand the new world and the technology which we older people cannot understand. Theirs is the future. The new struggle is longer and harder and touches everyone. But as with the struggle of resistance, the struggle for Independence, this struggle will also be won. The woman was strengthened by the war, and she will be strenghtened by the third struggle. The woman and the man, the people as a whole, will then be better, stronger and more content.

Let's face it: what we are struggling for is democratic rights for everyone. We are part of the struggle by the Third World as a whole, for freedom from want, poverty and hunger. This cannot be achieved in isolation. Women cannot struggle alone against male domination.

We have a government that is on the road to socialism. When the end of the road is reached, all class distinction will be abolished. Equality of sex can then be fully achieved. This is the hope, the aim, the goal.

Appendix i

The following extract from an article in the Rhodesian *Herald* (24 December, 1977), shows how the Rhodesians attempted to use the involvement of women in ZANLA to cast an unfavourable light on the freedom struggle.

Turning women into terrorists...

The Rhodesian authorities yesterday released some of the documents and photographs seized during the security forces' raid on Chimoio camp last month, in which more than 1,200 terrorists were reported to have been killed. The main emphasis of both documents and photographs was that women recruits of Mr Robert Mugabe's banned ZANU organisation were receiving military training at the Mozambique camp just north of what used to be Vila Pery.

One of the photographs showed the ZANU terrorists' commander, Mr Joshua Tongogara, instructing two women in the use of AK assault rifles. The remainder included:

— A platoon of women drilling with fixed bayonets;
— A group of women with SAR rifles being instructed before a blackboard on how to load and unload;
— Two women, one with a rocket launcher and the other with an AK, beside radio equipment;
— The terrorist leader, Mr Rex Nhongo, addressing a rally, with Mr Tongogara seated beside him.

One of the captured documents released yesterday was headed Zimbabwe African National Union (ZANU), ZANLA headquarters, Chimoio. It was dated June 6 this year and sub-headed Department of Personnel. It listed the home, name and Chimurenga (war) name of 80 women assigned 'on a mission to Manica Province'. This is a sample of the names, with the Chimurenga name in brackets:
Charity Munharira (Resistance Nhamoinesu),
Juliet Makondora (No-rest Muhondo),
Hellen Muchirahondo (Push-more Hondo), and
Donah Dhilwayo (Silent War).

The list is completed by the slogan, 'Forward with ZANU'. There is a further list of 114 Chimurenga names, many of them women, and three commanders. Against each name is listed a gun number and type of weapon, including one bazooka.

Another of the captured documents is part of the ZANU report of the Department of Administration to the first session of the enlarged Central Committee, Maputo, and dated August of this year. The section deals with the 'place and role of female comrades in the revolution'. The report reads:

Since the March-April Chimoio meeting at which two of our female comrades were appointed to positions in the Central Committee, the Department of Administration has been pleased to see continual efforts by the Executive Committee to get as many as possible of our women comrades to participate in more challenging and satisfying tasks.

But it must be pointed out that the ground is still insignificantly scratched. The party still badly needs to revolutionise its attitude to female comrades and urgently supervise the development and practice of a new attitude.

In the main, the great bulk of our female comrades are still regarded as good for nothing more than casual sex and beautiful company for male comrades. They quickly become unwanted burdens of the revolution when they become pregnant.

There is an overwhelming reluctance to invite and challenge female comrades to the more significant tasks of the revolution. Male comrades still think it humiliating to salute their senior-ranking female comrades. Our female comrades are also to blame. Many are still just 'women' in the old traditional sense. They still think it is anathema for them to take up the challenge of the revolution on an equal footing with male comrades. Many have ambitions to live to the peak of a loose moral life through the revolution.

The party badly needs to define with much greater exactness, what role the women of Zimbabwe must play along the path of the revolution....'

Appendix ii

Important Events

1200   The construction of Great Zimbabwe; founding of Zimbabwe Empire.

1500   The establishment of Mutapa Empire; trade with Arabs, later with Portuguese, evolves; Portuguese introduce maize into the region.

1569   Start of a hundred years conflict with Portuguese, hastening the fragmentation of the Shona peoples.

1839   Arrival of the Ndebele under Chief Mzilkazi in the southern region, subsequently named Matabeleland.

1888   Signing of concessions for mining rights for the British South Africa Company by the Ndebele King, Lobengula.

1890   Arrival of BSAC Pioneer Column and its occupation of Mashonaland.

1893   Uprising and defeat of the Ndebele and occupation of Matabeleland by BSAC.

1895   Matabeleland and Mashonaland named 'Rhodesia'.

1896/7   Revolt of Shona and Ndebele; Ndebele defeated October 1896, Shona in 1897.

1898   Nehanda and Kaguvi, spirit mediums involved in the 1896/7 uprising are executed; Rhodesia becomes the Colony of Southern Rhodesia.

1919   London rules that all land in the Colony belonged to the Crown.

1923   End of BSAC rule; Southern Rhodesia becomes a self-governing colony.

1930   Land Aportionment Act allocates land between Africans and Europeans.

1934   African National Congress formed.

1951   Land Husbandry Act forces culling of African cattle.

1953   Central African Federation formed between Southern Rhodesia, Northern Rhodesia, Nyasaland (Zimbabwe, Zambia, Malawi).

1955   African National Youth League formed; law passed introducing detention without trial.

1957   Youth League and African National Congress merge; Joshua Nkomo becomes ANC President.

1959   ANC banned.

1960   A successor party, the National Democratic Party (NDP), formed.

1961   NDP banned; succeeded by Zimbabwe African People's Union (ZAPU). New constitution proposed; Nkomo first accepts then repudiates proposals.

1962   ZAPU banned. Rhodesian Front Party formed and wins elections.

1963   Central African Federation dissolved. Nationalist movement split by formation of a new party, Zimbabwe African National Union, under the Rev. Ndabaningi Sithole. Nkomo forms People's Caretaker Party (PCP).

1964   Ian Smith becomes Prime Minister. ZANU and PCP banned. Leaders and members detained include Nkomo, Sithole and Mugabe.

1965   Smith declared Rhodesia's independence illegally (UDI — Unilateral Declaration of Independence). UK applies sanctions. First guerrillas enter the country (ZANLA/ZIPRA). State of Emergency proclaimed.

1966   Mandatory sanctions by the United Nations. Harold Wilson meets Smith on board HMS Tiger. Battle of Sinoia marks the start of guerrilla war.

1968   Another Wilson-Smith meeting, on board HMS Fearless. UN applies total mandatory sanctions.

1970   Rhodesia declares itself a Republic.

1971   British settlement terms accepted by Smith. Bishop Abel Muzorewa forms African National Council (ANC).

1972   African majority reject settlement terms, following an ANC 'no' campaign; Pearce Commission reports result back to London.
        New phase of war with the opening of a front on the north-eastern border by guerrillas of the Zimbabwe African National Liberation Army (ZANLA), the military wing of ZANU.

1973   Border closed between Rhodesia and Zambia. Smith starts talks with Muzorewa.

1974   Coup in Lisbon changes balance of power in Southern Africa. Zambia and Pretoria begin detente contacts. Smith forced to release detained leaders who signed Unity Accord in Lusaka (Muzorewa, Sithole, Nkomo, James Chikerema).

1975   ZANU's leader in exile, Herbert Chitepo, is murdered. Meeting between Smith and Zimbabwean leaders on the Victoria Falls railway bridge.

1976   Guerrilla war intensifies. Henry Kissinger shuttles around Southern Africa, forces Smith to concede need for majority rule. Nkomo and Mugabe form Patriotic Front Alliance. Abortive conference chaired by Britain is held in Geneva, with Smith, Muzorewa, Nkomo and Mugabe (now spokesman for ZANU).

1977   Britain launches new initiative together with the US. Rhodesia attacks refugee camps in Mozambique.

1978   Anglo-American initiates a meeting in Malta with Patriotic Front; Smith works out 'internal solution' by agreement with Muzorewa, Sithole and Chief Chirau. Transitional government formed. Rhodesia attacks targets in Zambia.

1979   Muzorewa victorious in election, becomes Prime Minister. Margaret Thatcher at Lusaka Commonwealth Conference agrees to hold constitutional conference.

Lancaster House talks start 10 September, ending with cease-fire agreement effective from 21 December. British governor sent to Salisbury on 12 December.

1980   March elections end with victory for ZANU (57 seats); Nkomo wins 20 seats, Muzorewa 3. Twenty White seats entrenched for limited period. On 18 April, Rhodesia became the Republic of Zimbabwe.